The United States and the Cold War 1941-53

Richard Crockatt

British Associa

First Published 1989

© British Association for American Studies, 1989

ISBN 0 946488 08 8

ACKNOWLEDGEMENTS

The maps on page 26 and page 42 were drawn by K. J. Wass and first published in Paul Hastings, *The Cold War 1945-69* (London: Ernest Benn, 1969). They are reproduced here by kind permission of Ernest Benn, Ltd.

Printed by the University of Sussex Printing Unit, Falmer, Brighton BN1 9RH, East Sussex. Telephone: (0273) 606755.

Contents

		Page
I	**Perspectives on the Cold War**	7
	Historians and the Cold War	7
	The American and Soviet Foreign Policy Traditions	12
II	**Endings and Beginnings 1941-1946**	15
	The Grand Alliance	15
	The Breakdown of the Alliance	17
	1946: The Turning Point	22
III	**Containment and the Division of Europe**	27
	The Truman Doctrine	28
	The Marshall Plan, Germany, and the Division of Europe	30
	NATO, NSC-68 and the Militarization of Containment	33
IV	**Cold War in the Far East**	35
	McCarthyism and the Far Eastern Turn	35
	China, Japan and the Ferment in Asia	37
	The Korean War	41
V	**Conclusion**	45
	Notes	47
	Guide to Further Reading	51

CHRONOLOGY

1941

July	Germany invades Russia
December	Japanese attack on Pearl Harbor
	US enters the war

1943

November	Teheran Conference
	Dissolution of the Comintern

1944

June 6	Normandy landings

1945

February	Yalta Conference
April 11	Death of Roosevelt, succeeded by Truman
May 8	Allied victory in Europe
July-August	Potsdam Conference
August 15	Japanese surrender following Hiroshima (August 6) and Nagasaki (August 9)

1946

February 9	Stalin's election speech
February 22	Kennan's 'Long Telegram'
February 28	Byrnes's hard line with the Soviets speech
March 5	Churchill's 'Iron Curtain' speech at Fulton, Missouri
March-April	Iranian crisis
September 12	Wallace's speech on US-Soviet relations and resignation

1947

January	British and American occupation zones in Germany
March 15	joined Truman Doctrine speech
June 5	Marshall's speech announcing European Recovery Program
July	Kennan's article 'The Sources of Soviet Conduct'
October	Creation of Cominform

1948

February	Communist coup in Czechoslovakia
March	Congress adopts Marshall Plan
June	Tito expelled from Cominform
	Beginning of Berlin Blockade

CHRONOLOGY (continued)

1949

April	NATO Treaty signed
May	Berlin blockade ended
	Federal Republic of Germany established
September	News of Soviet atomic bomb test released in US
October	People's Republic of China proclaimed in Peking
December	Chiang Kai-shek flees to Formosa
	German Democratic Republic established

1950

January	Alger Hiss convicted of perjury
	Acheson's Asian defense perimeter speech
February	McCarthy's first major anti-communist speech
June	North Korean invasion of South Korea
October	China enters the Korean War

1951

April	Truman dismisses MacArthur
September	Japanese Peace Treaty signed

1952 Eisenhower elected to presidency

1953

March	Death of Stalin
July	Korean armistice signed

1 Perspectives on the Cold War

Historians and the Cold War

After a generation and more of intensive research, historians are no nearer agreement on the causes of the Cold War than they are on other subjects of major importance. To the familiar problem of all historical inquiry — the susceptibility of evidence to multiple interpretations — must be added the decisive fact that the Cold War is a going concern. Total detachment in these circumstances is a sheer impossibility. The passage of time nevertheless can reshape conceptions of even the recent past. The advent of Secretary Gorbachev to the leadership of the Soviet Union, for example, can serve as a triangulation point for a remapping of the postwar years. It allows us to see Soviet foreign policies over the whole period less as an outgrowth of a single species of communism than as a complex interplay between internal and external pressures. That Soviet communism has the potential to change in important ways throws the Stalinist era, for example, into sharper relief. It is now revealed more clearly than ever before as a particular phase in the development of the Soviet state.[1] The same holds true for the United States, though arguably to a lesser degree. Ronald Reagan's presidency was in many respects a throw-back to the early years of the Cold War. Certainly Americans as a whole have been less inclined to echo recent Soviet views that in the era of 'glasnost' the Cold War is over. Nevertheless, for most American historians, if not for officials in the administration, the beginnings of the Cold War are by now in a real sense 'history'.

Interpretation of the origins of the Cold War hinges on three issues: [assessment of the motives behind American foreign policy, the motives of Soviet policy, and some conception of how nations interact.] Clearly the lack of primary sources for the study of the Soviet Union, when compared with the reams of American documents, creates a special problem. There are often few means of testing assumptions about Soviet policy against evidence, with the result that conclusions are frequently based on speculation. Memoirs and documents do, however, exist, selective and partial though these are. We also have the record of Soviet actions themselves. Given that this is the evidence with which American policy-makers were confronted, historians must likewise give it close attention. Besides, the massive and growing bulk of American sources has by no means settled the question of the motives of American policy-makers and there is no reason to think that a comparable mass of Soviet sources would make unanimity among historians any more likely. A serious information gap nevertheless exists on the Soviet side and is likely to continue for the foreseeable future. Despite signs of changing attitudes in the Soviet Union, fully informed debate on Soviet policies remains impossible.

American historiography of the Cold War is frequently categorized according to 'orthodoxy', 'revisionism', and 'post-revisionism', appearing in succession roughly in the 1950s, 1960s and 1970s in line with political developments at home and abroad. Consensus among American historians on the nature of the Soviet threat and on America's firm response to it in the 1940s and 1950s (orthodoxy) gave way to criticism of US policy in the era of Vietnam (revisionism), to be replaced by the less politically charged writings of the détente years (post-revisionism). There is some justice in this scheme. Historians have undoubtedly reflected the prevailing climates of opinion in their work. Neither the climates of opinion nor the historians' responses to them, however, have been as simple as this scheme would suggest. In the first place, vigorous debate took place within each historiographical phase. There was, for example, no single entity called orthodoxy. Secondly, earlier views were not abandoned as new ones appeared. The historiography of the Cold War has been a continuing conversation in which the number of participants has increased without silencing all the previous voices. What has changed over the years is the relative weight ascribed by historians to the three points mentioned above as the central foci of debate: Soviet intentions, American intentions, and the interaction between them.

The first generation of analysts of the Cold War was heavily influenced by the singular condition of the early postwar years: the emergence of a bipolar divide between two superpowers based on antagonistic social and political principles. Bipolarity was a novel condition in international relations and presented a sharp challenge to those whose assumptions about international affairs were formed in the prewar era when power was distributed among a number of nations. Moreover, the emergence of bipolarity went along with, indeed was a consequence of, the displacement of the old Great Powers of Europe as the focus of the world system. It posed the problem of explaining and justifying the assumption of a new world role by the United States. The so-called 'orthodox' position on the Cold War is in actuality a complex of views which range from simple endorsement of government policy to more or less stringent criticisms of it. What links them is broad acceptance of the view that an expanded US world role was an inevitable product of circumstances, chief among these being the collapse of the old centres of power and the actual or threatened entrance of the Soviet Union into the gap, not only in Europe but also in the Near, Middle and Far East where the old powers had previously exerted influence.

Within the framework of orthodoxy one can identify 'ideologists' and 'realists'. The former, such as political scientist Zbigniew Brzezinski (later National Security Adviser under President Carter), saw the Soviet Union as driven by militant ideological expansionism which could be met only by vigorous American counter-measures. Writing in 1960, he saw little prospect of moderation in Soviet goals and hence little chance of peaceful coexistence with the Kremlin.[2] Traditional displomacy was hardly possible in these circumstances since the Soviet Union did not subscribe to its values and traditions. Realists by contrast not only believed that Soviet actions arose as much from the desire for security as from ideology but that America's own tradition of moralistic diplomacy was ill-suited to cope with the postwar world. Americans did not understand the factor of power in international relations. With their all-or-nothing approach, wrote John Spanier in a widely used survey of American foreign policy published in 1960, Americans tended 'either to abstain from the dirty game of power politics or to crusade for its complete elimination'. This posture, furthermore, militated 'against the use of diplomacy in its classical sense: to compromise interests, to conciliate differences, and to moderate and isolate conflicts'. George Kennan, a prominent American diplomat and historian, declared in 1950 that 'a good deal of our trouble seems to have stemmed from the extent to which the executive has felt itself beholden to short-term trends of public opinion in the country and from what we might call the erratic and subjective nature of public reaction to foreign-policy questions'.[3]

The realists' critique of American policy stopped short of total condemnation. Their quarrel was with the style rather than the substance of American diplomacy since they had few doubts that a Soviet threat existed which must be met. It is sometimes claimed that the roots of revisionism are to be found in realist writings of the 1940s and 1950s, particularly those of the prominent journalist Walter Lippmann. Lippmann himself, though on occasions a sharp critic of administration policies, repudiated the suggestion, and with good reason.[4] Revisionists by and large shared neither the realists' assumptions about power nor their broad endorsement of President Truman's policies towards the Soviet Union. Revisionists such as William Appleman Williams and Gabriel Kolko were in many respects closer to the orthodox ideologists than to the realists in that they reinstated ideology as the central category of analysis. They simply shifted attention to American rather than Soviet ideology.[5]

The revisionist critique was most powerfully mounted by William Appleman Williams' *Tragedy of American Diplomacy* (1st edition 1959). His basic propositions were that the United States had instigated the Cold War and that Soviet policies had been fundamentally defensive and limited in scope. The ideology of American capitalism, expressed as the pursuit of an 'open door' or expanding market for American goods, was, he argued, the determining force behind American diplomacy. Fear of a depression haunted American leaders and drove them to seek outlets for surplus production. Not all revisionists followed Williams along this line of interpretation. Some placed emphasis on personalities (particularly of Truman) and on strident anti-communism in their explanations of the 'get tough' American policies of the early postwar years.[6] One important link, however, between revisionists of whatever type was the view that the Cold War had resulted essentially from unilateral American actions and that it had therefore been an avoidable tragedy.

The Vietnam War and its domestic repercussions undoubtedly served to bring revisionism close to the centre of historiographical debate about the origins of the Cold War. It explains in part why the focus of revisionist histories was on American rather than Soviet policy. The central issue was conceived to be: how had the United States arrived at the point where it had become the citadel of reaction and the opponent of freedom movements around the world? In this respect revisionism was no less affected by the agenda of national and international politics than was orthodoxy. However, although the agenda has changed since the appearance of the pioneering works of revisionism, revisionism remains a powerful force and has been developed and refined in important ways.[7]

Both the altered agenda and the continuing influence of revisionism are discernible in a third historiographical phase, which can be usefully dated from the publication in 1972 of John Lewis Gaddis's *The United States and the Origins of the Cold War, 1941-1947*. This group of historians, generally labelled 'post-revisionist', has been markedly diverse in approach and conclusions. This is so not merely because the winding down of the Vietnam War and the emergence of détente in the early 1970s introduced greater diffuseness into the foreign policy debate but because a mass of new sources became available. These included documents made accessible by the passage of the Freedom of Information Act in 1974. The result has been to enlarge the focus of historiographical inquiry and in some respects to blur the outlines of US-Soviet relations supplied by previous interpreters.

Historians such as Gaddis acknowledge the value of the revisionists' attention to economic factors in American policy-making without, however, accepting the view that these were decisive. Economic factors are seen rather in the context of an array of domestic constraints which limited policy options in crucial ways. The picture which emerges is of an America struggling to reconcile its heritage of isolationism with the pressure to assume a leading role in the growing conflict with the Soviet Union. Unlike the revisionists, who saw American leaders pursuing a consistent and assertive line towards the Soviet Union from the middle of 1945, Gaddis and other post-revisionists are struck by the hesitancy with which America adopted its unprecedentedly active role in peacetime world affairs. Gaddis, however, can be said to have restored an element of the orthodox interpretation in his view that the Soviet Union bore primary responsibility for the breakdown of the wartime alliance.[8] Daniel Yergin, another prominent post-revisionist, by contrast owes more to revisionism than to orthodoxy in his critical analysis of Truman's abandonment of cooperation with the Soviet Union.[9]

A significant new departure in recent discussions of the Cold War has been the close attention given to British policy. A number of historians, many of them British, have suggested that in the decisive period from mid-1945 to early 1946 Britain's contribution was to awaken the United States to the reality of the Soviet threat and that the United States had to be coaxed into its role of Western leadership. From this perspective the central theme of the early Cold War was Anglo-Soviet conflict, in which the United States sought initially to play a mediating role. The failure of British efforts in 1944-45 to create an Anglo-Soviet alliance, coupled with Britain's serious financial problems in the postwar years, forced the United States to assume a role which Britain was no longer capable of fulfilling — that of guarantor of stability in Western Europe, Iran, and Turkey.[10] This interpretation evidently complements Gaddis's account and it has also qualified the revisionist argument that the United States rode roughshod over Britain's interests in pursuit of economic and political hegemony. In short, post-revisionist accounts, while addressing some of the arguments put forward by revisionists and in many instances acknowledging revisionism's contribution, have tended to argue for the primacy of the political over the economic and of multi-causal over mono-causal explanations.

It will be apparent from this brief review that it is no easy matter to keep analysis of Soviet and American intentions and their interaction in balance. Ideological interpretations, whether orthodox or revisionist, tend to operate with a double standard. Orthodox historians attribute American policy to a concern with national security and Soviet policy to limitless ideological goals, while revisionists employ the same scheme in reverse. Both view the Cold War as essentially the consequence of one power acting upon another. Both adopt 'total' explanations which make it difficult to account for specific policies which do not fit into the favoured scheme. Orthodox historians interpret signs of pragmatism in Stalin's policies — such as his unwillingness to support the communist rebels in the Greek Civil War between 1944 and 1947 — as merely tactical moves in the service of a larger plan to extend the sphere of Soviet domination. Revisionists iron out inconsistencies in American policy by recourse to the open door thesis. The Marshall Plan of 1947, which sought the economic reconstruction of Western Europe, was opposed by many Republicans in Congress and by business interests as involving a wasteful expenditure of American resources. It was labelled contemptuously, in reference to Franklin Roosevelt's despised 'New Deal' policies of the 1930s, as a 'New Deal for Europe'. In the event the Plan was endorsed by Congress only after the communist coup in Czechoslovakia (1948) provoked a sense of crisis and a consensus had emerged on the means of dealing with it. Even then, the administration's original requests were pared down by a cost-conscious Congress. In this instance and many others it is difficult to discern any simple fit between ideology and policy outcomes. Revisionist accounts also ignore the extent to which pressure for US involvement in the economic affairs of Western Europe came from the Europeans themselves.

Revisionism, however, was never merely an inversion of orthodoxy. Its emphasis on economic factors was an important corrective to the exclusive concern in orthodox writings with politics and diplomacy. This weakness in orthodox histories applies not only to the ideologists but also to the realists, for all their seductive hard-headedness. Revisionists have rightly indicated the degree to which the outward thrust of American policy was a consequence of the inherent dynamism of the American economy, even if they have pursued this argument to excessive lengths. Post-revisionists such as Gaddis and Yergin have gone some way towards meeting the problems raised in both orthodox and revisionist histories by directing close attention to the *processes* of American policy-making, which, it now seems clear, were complex and often contradictory. Their emphasis on wartime diplomacy, furthermore, has helped to place American Cold War policies more fully within the context of the global crisis of the Second World War. The problem of assessing Soviet intentions remains. An explanation of American diplomacy does not of itself account for the Cold War, as Gaddis acknowledges.[11] In the absence of definitive answers to the question of Soviet intentions and to the other questions raised in these pages, one can at least strive to accord due weight to the factors in US-Soviet conflict as they were perceived and acted upon by both sides.

The American and Soviet Foreign Policy Traditions

The American foreign policy tradition is the product of a revolutionary heritage and geographical location. The Revolution supplied America with a set of principles; physical isolation from Europe and the possession of vast territory available for expansion provided the means of preserving and subsequently extending the range of its revolutionary principles. America's famed 'isolationist' tradition during the nineteenth century was in fact contingent upon physical distance from Europe and favourable economic conditions. Isolationism scarcely applied to Latin America. The Monroe Doctrine of 1823 embodied two claims: denial of the right of European Powers to attempt further colonization there, and an assertion of the incompatibility of the political values of the Old World and the New. America was different, yet representative of universal values. The Declaration of Independence, wrote President Lincoln, promised 'liberty, not alone to the people of this country, but hope for the world for all future time'.[12]

As the United States entered the twentieth century and overtook the major European nations in economic power, the sense of difference was retained but its application in new circumstances elevated a hemispheric doctrine to a global scale. Breaking with the isolationist tradition in 1917 to enter the First World War, President Wilson announced that America was going to war 'to make the world safe for democracy'. What has been called the 'diplomacy of principle'[13] was not merely a matter of couching policy in idealistic terms. It was the product of a culture which had experienced revolution and national growth as a 'natural' process. America had achieved revolution in the late eighteenth century, as Louis Hartz has observed, without a major class upheaval.[14] It had expanded across the continent without damaging conflicts with major powers. It had achieved economic growth, so it was believed, through the natural operations of the market. What more logical than to assume that liberal democracy, laissez-faire economics, and a diplomacy based on the application of self-evident principles should suffice for all nations? The difficulty experienced by the United States in accepting the consequences of twentieth-century revolutions was thus rooted in its cultural tradition. To compromise with those revolutions was to betray America's own.

The germ of the Cold War lies in the coincidence of Woodrow Wilson's globalism and the Bolshevik Revolution of October 1917. Ironically both Wilson and Lenin consciously dissociated themselves from the diplomacy of the European powers. Secret diplomacy, annexations, trade discrimination, exclusive alliances (the United States entered the war as an 'associated', not an allied power) and balance of power politics were denounced as generators of war. Both leaders, as Geoffrey Barraclough has pointed out, adopted a new democratic diplomacy, appealing to the people of other nations over the heads of politicians. Both were competing 'for the suffrage of mankind'.[15] They were competing, of course, on behalf of different ideologies, and relations quickly deteriorated as Lenin took Russia out of the war against Germany and the United States joined with other Western powers in a policy of intervention in Russia. That the aim, at least nominally, was to protect Western interests in Russia rather than unseat the Bolsheviks did not erase the Soviets' conviction that the United States was out to strangle the Revolution in its cradle.

These events illustrate clearly an important difference between the revolutionary experiences of the United States and the Soviet Union. From the outset the Soviet Union was under siege, forced to establish itself without the luxury of time and space to develop. Soviet policy, like that of the United States, thus arose not only from the dictates of ideology, but from the specific conditions of national growth. A preoccupation with security was inseparable from preservation of the Revolution and the furtherance of its goals. It is this which makes it difficult to accept the facile distinction often made between security and ideological expansion as motives behind Soviet foreign policy. To be sure, the Soviet Union often found it necessary to compromise. The Leninist goal of world revolution gave way to Stalin's 'socialism in the one country' as the hoped-for communist revolutions in Europe failed to materalize in the wake of the Bolshevik success. In the greatest compromise of all the Soviet Union signed a non-aggression pact with Nazi Germany in 1939 in the hope that German aggression would be directed westwards rather than eastwards. Both of these instances, however, are compatible with the view that ideology and national interest were inextricably mixed in Soviet policy. The Soviet Union did not abandon the goal of promoting communism wherever possible during the period of 'socialism in one country'. During the period of the Nazi-Soviet pact (1939-41) the Soviet Union took the opportunity to absorb and sovietize Eastern Poland and the Baltic States, and to attack Finland. These examples show that the Soviet Union was capable of flexibility in the short term in the service of long-term goals, arguably to a greater degree than the United States. But they also suggest that Russian nationalism and Soviet communism were two sides of the same coin.

Two revolutions, two states with explicit principles at stake, two large nations with expansive tendencies: these do not of themselves make for Cold War. While its beginnings can be discerned in the years 1917-1920, it took another world war and an alliance between the United States and the Soviet Union to ignite the Cold War proper. In the interwar years the decisive factors in international relations were the efforts of Germany and Japan to reorder the balance of power in their favour within their respective spheres. Until the late 1930s the United States played a peripheral role in these dramas, while the Soviet Union, more directly threatened by German resurgence, attempted a holding action, first by the promotion of collective security via the League of Nations and second, when that failed, by entering into a short-lived agreement with Germany in the form of the

Nazi-Soviet Pact of August 1939. Throughout the 1930s relations between the United States and the Soviet Union themselves were cool, despite American diplomatic recognition of the Soviet Union on Franklin Roosevelt's assumption of the presidency. Relations were also distant. There were neither major areas of agreement nor pressing conflicts of interest.

The war changed that picture out of all recognition. Agreement within the 'Grand Alliance' on the goal of defeating Germany (the Soviet Union did not declare war on Japan until August 1945) and the achievement of that goal in May 1945 left Europe at the disposal of the victorious powers but it also placed a high premium on the continuance of unity if a postwar settlement was to succeed. As we know, Great Power unity broke down. The Cold War was thus in important respects an outgrowth of the Second World War. The latent ideological antagonism stemming from 1917 was, so to speak, energized by the demands placed upon the United States and the Soviet Union for cooperation during the war and its aftermath.

II Endings and Beginnings 1941-46

The Grand Alliance

How cooperative was the Grand Alliance? The Roosevelt administration certainly made efforts to present 'our gallant ally' in a favourable light to American public opinion. Roosevelt made long trips to meet Stalin at Teheran in 1943 and Yalta in 1945 at considerable risk to his health and security. Even before America entered the war, lend-lease aid was made available to the Soviet Union. Beyond that, Roosevelt indicated repeatedly his desire for cooperation to the fullest extent possible in both the political and military spheres. The decision to pursue a Europe-first strategy rather than concentrate the American effort on defeating her attacker Japan was in part prompted by Roosevelt's awareness that the Soviet Union was bearing the major military and civilian burden of the war. Stalin, while making clear his paramount interest in the establishment of friendly governments on Russia's western border following the war, gave at least nominal assent to the principles of the Atlantic Charter (1941) and the Declaration on Liberated Europe (1945), among whose provisions was self-determination for all peoples. The dismantling in 1943 of the Comintern (the international arm of the Soviet Communist Party) was presented by the Soviet Union and perceived in the West as a gesture of goodwill, implying a suspension of the ideological goal of spreading communism.[16] Finally, Stalin indicated that he would go along with Roosevelt's cherished idea of a United Nations Organization to replace the old League of Nations.

Strained relations, however, were evident from an early stage in the war, and given the fact that the Alliance was largely a marriage of convenience this was hardly surprising. Two issues loomed large. The first was Stalin's request for acknowledgement of Soviet interests in Eastern Europe (essentially a ratification of the gains Stalin had acquired in the Nazi-Soviet Pact of 1939, above all the Baltic states and eastern Poland). The Western Allies resisted making firm commitments on this point at the outset of the Alliance and Stalin reluctantly agreed to postpone agreement upon receipt of an assurance that the Western Allies would mount a 'second front' in Western Europe with all speed. This became a second point of friction since the major assault in North-West Europe which Stalin desired was repeatedly postponed, preeminently at Churchill's insistence, until June 1944. (Indeed differences between Roosevelt and Churchill on strategy formed a powerful cross-current in the wartime Alliance, with Churchill less inclined than Roosevelt to yield to Soviet interests and doggedly insistent on protecting British interests in the Near East — hence his preference for a Mediterranean rather than a Northern European strategy.) The reason for delay offered by Churchill and Roosevelt was that their military preparations were not sufficiently advanced to ensure success. The Western Allies settled instead on a North African campaign in 1942 followed in 1943 by landings in Sicily and the Italian mainland. Stalin's suspicion of bad faith on the part of the Western Allies proved to be a potent source of mistrust, full of praise though he was for the Allied landings in France when they finally came.

A pattern was set in which military decisions would come to have major political repercussions. Roosevelt's policy was not, as has sometimes been claimed, to ignore political issues in favour of military priorities. While it is true that he preferred to leave detailed discussion of territorial questions until the German surrender was within sight, he had clear political motives for doing so. Chief among these was his conviction that the best foundation for postwar reconstruction lay in the continuance of big power unity and that depended, in his view, on the swift prosecution of the war to a successful military conclusion. To press forward on territorial issues too early, above all on Eastern Europe, would be to risk exposing serious differences between the Western Allies and Stalin. In any case Roosevelt had little quarrel with the general proposition that the Soviet Union was justified in seeking friendly governments on its western border. He would doubtless, though, have been less sanguine about the chances of avoiding a wholesale Soviet domination of Eastern Europe if he had been able to overhear Stalin's remark to Milovan Djilas in early 1945 to the effect that 'this war is not as in the past: whoever occupies a territory also imposes his own system as far as his army can reach'.[17]

By the time Roosevelt, Churchill, and Stalin gathered at Yalta in the Soviet Crimea in February 1945 to discuss the major questions arising from the imminent prospect of victory over Germany, the broad framework of the territorial arrangements had been decided by the disposition of forces. The American decision not to engage in a race with the Russians for Berlin and to allow Soviet troops to take Prague, decisions made partly on military and partly on political grounds, reinforced the emerging pattern of divided responsibility between zones of occupation. The Western Allies themselves had already set a precedent in Italy where the Allied Control Council, on which a Soviet representative sat, was accorded only advisory status, the real power lying with the Western Allied commander of the occupying force. The more comprehensive European Advisory Commission, charged with overseeing joint military and political control of all liberated areas, was similarly limited in its capacity to enforce a unified approach in the treatment of liberated areas.

The Breakdown of the Alliance

The subsequent breakdown in the Grand Alliance can be traced through the year following V-E day (May 8, 1945) in the attempts to deal with an array of major problems: the establishment of a new political order via the United Nations Organization, the reconstruction of the world economy, the settlement of borders and the establishment of new governments in Poland and Eastern Europe, the treatment of Germany, and the issue of atomic energy. By the middle of 1946 the mould was set in which the best that could be achieved on each of these issues was fragile agreement; the worst was rank failure to find common ground.

On the face of it the United Nations represents the least unsuccessful joint venture of the postwar years. Having repudiated Woodrow Wilson's cherished League of Nations in 1919, the United States was now determined to play a leading role in the new international organization. Bipartisan support in Congress for participation and widespread public sentiment in favour of internationalism were decisive in making up Roosevelt's mind. Not that this meant a reversion to the Wilsonian idealism of 1919. Convinced that the League of Nations had been based on the unrealistic assumption that all nations deserved equal status in decision-making, Roosevelt favoured Big Power predominance. This priority was reflected in the Dumbarton Oaks Plan of 1944 in which preeminent power was given to the Security Council with its five permanent members — The United States, The Soviet Union, Great Britain, France, and China —while the 'universalist' principle of the old League of Nations was retained in the form of the Assembly. Stalin, though less inclined to trust Soviet interests to an international body, was prepared to countenance a scheme which acknowledged the reality that some powers were more equal than others. The organization was thus conceived essentially as a continuation of the wartime alliance.

Early disputes arose over procedural issues and the Soviet Union's claim to sixteen votes in the Assembly, based on its sixteen 'autonomous republics' and designed to match the separate votes accorded to the nations within the British Empire. Agreement on these points, however, scarcely removed crippling weaknesses from the organization. The veto power available to the five permanent members of the Security Council, desired as much by the United States as by the Soviet Union, meant that each could forestall decisions perceived to be against its interests. In so far as the effectiveness of the organization depended upon Big Power unity, disagreement on major issues would undermine its capacity to act. Such proved to be the case. The UN became a mirror of the growing disunity among the major powers. Its singular 'success' in the early postwar years, the decision to resist the North Korean invasion of South Korea in June 1950, was possible because at the time the Soviet Union was boycotting the organization in protest at the refusal of the UN to admit Mao Tse-Tung's government as the legitimate government of China. (The nationalist government of Chiang Kai-shek had been driven out to the island of Formosa in 1949.)

Cooperation to promote a new economic order proved even more elusive. The Roosevelt administration was convinced that the political instability of the interwar years had been rooted in economic nationalism and had been a major cause of the Second World War. Roosevelt's closest advisers believed therefore, in the words of Treasury official Harry Dexter White, that 'the absence of a high degree of economic collaboration among the leading nations, will, during the coming decade. inevitably result in economic warfare that will be but the prelude and instigator of military warfare on an even vaster scale'.[18] The outcome was the formulation at Bretton Woods in 1944 of a plan to provide for international currency stabilization and the distribution of loans to needy countries with a view to promoting international trade. The key principle as far as the United States was concerned was openness, its global applicability to capitalist and communist states alike. Indeed the United States anticipated more resistance from Britain, with its jealously guarded system of imperial preference, than from the Soviet Union. Economic self-interest undoubtedly played a large role in the United States's promotion of the system. As by far the largest subscriber of funds to the proposed International Monetary Fund and the World Bank, the United States was in a position to determine the shape and the operation of the new institutions. It stood to gain from an increased demand for American exports and from the shifting of financial and commercial power to the United States. It was also thought that the new system would obviate the need for large-scale US loans to other countries for postwar reconstruction.

In practice, while the United States did become the world's economic and financial powerhouse, this was less because of the establishment of the Bretton Woods machinery than because of the simple fact that the United States emerged from the war as the dominant and expanding economic power. The Bretton Woods system of itself was not capable of creating economic equilibrium where no equilibrium existed, and extensive loans to Britain and later to Western Europe as a whole via the Marshall Plan proved necessary. The Soviet Union meanwhile, having endorsed the Bretton Woods agreements in 1944, failed to ratify the accords by the deadline of December 31, 1945. This decision seems to have arisen less from objections to the plan itself than from growing rifts with the United States on other issues during 1945. The American refusal to grant a postwar loan without stringent conditions, involving access for American goods and investment to the Soviet Union, exacerbated relations which were already marked by serious disputes over the formation of governments in Eastern Europe. In this sense, as John Gaddis has remarked, the Soviets' withdrawal from participation in the Bretton Woods system 'was an effect rather than a cause of the cold war'.[19] Nevertheless, the result was to encourage the development of separate economic blocs to match the political divisions which were fast appearing.

Confrontation over the establishment of new governments in Poland and other East European countries, coupled with the failure to agree on a German settlement, lay at the heart of the emerging Cold War. Agreements of a sort, however, were reached on Eastern Europe and to that extent tension arose as much from problems of interpretation and implementation of agreed policies as over the character of the policies themselves. On Poland provision was made at Yalta for the establishment of a new government based on the existing Soviet-backed 'Lublin' government but with the addition of 'democratic leaders from Poland and from Poles abroad'. Free elections were to follow as soon as the military situation would permit. Even before FDR's death on April 8, 1945 wrangles had developed over observance of the agreement, as the Soviet Union made it clear that it was unprepared either to accord non-Communists any real role or to conduct the kind of elections which would satisfy the West. Roosevelt's successor, Harry Truman, introduced a more abrasive style in relations with the Soviet Union, but in substance he sought to continue Roosevelt's preference for dealing independently with Stalin rather than tying America to British policy and arousing Stalin's suspicions of a Western Allied bloc against him. Truman dispatched Harry Hopkins, a former Roosevelt advisor, to Moscow in May 1945 in an effort to persuade Stalin to make good the Yalta pledges on Poland. The meeting produced minor Soviet concessions, enough to lead the United States to recognize the new Polish government, but in essence little had changed. The truth was that Truman was left with the alternative of accepting an unsatisfactory agreement or provoking an open breach with Stalin.

A similar pattern followed in Rumania and Bulgaria. In a series of Foreign Ministers' conferences held in late 1945, during which Stalin managed to exploit disagreements between the United States and Britain, a framework was established for settlements on Bulgaria and Rumania. These provided nominal self-government but little in the way of genuine democracy. Only in Czechoslovakia and Hungary did non-communists still retain real power but, as events were to prove, the United States possessed as little leverage in those countries as they did in Bulgaria and Rumania. (This is discussed in Chapter III.) An important result of the tangled and often acrimonious negotiations over Eastern Europe was to draw the United States and Britain closer together. British objections that American Secretary of State James Byrnes was willing to pay too high a price for agreement with Stalin, coupled with criticism within the United States of the agreements on Bulgaria and Rumania, provoked a reassessment of American policy towards the Soviet Union. By early 1946 a new and tougher American line was developing, characterized by a growing partnership between the United States and Britain. Whether more coordinated policies at an earlier date would have made a material difference to the situation in Eastern Europe, however, is doubtful. The extent to which the time for bargaining was past is well brought out in a frank remark by Maxim Litvinov to the American journalist Edgar Snow as early as June 1945: 'Why did you Americans wait till now to begin opposing us in the Balkans and Eastern Europe? . . . You should have done this three years ago. Now it's too late and your complaints only arouse suspicion now'.[20]

In Germany, American policy shifted from an initial desire to reduce that nation to virtual political and economic impotence to a recognition that an impoverished and resentful Germany could prove a potent source of instability in Europe. The Soviet Union's paramount interest — shared by France — in preventing German resurgence and gaining recompense for the destruction Germany had wreaked ran counter to the United States's growing preference for 'rehabilitation' over 'repression'.[21] Once again the issue of joint control by the Big Powers was the focus of disagreement. By 1944 zonal boundaries of occupation had been agreed, though within a framework of joint supervision of Germany as a single unit. The story of the following two years is of the hardening of these temporary zones of occupation into rigid boundaries.

Of the many disputed questions reparations posed the largest difficulty. Given its enormous human and material sacrifices in the war against Germany — it is estimated that the Soviet Union suffered 20 million casualties during the war — the Soviet Union had most at stake and at Yalta proposed the substantial sum of $20 billion as a basis for the joint Allied claim on Germany, half to go to the Soviet Union. Fearful of German economic collapse (and of the drain on the American taxpayer once the bill for German recovery was presented), the United States proposed instead at the Potsdam meeting in July 1945 that the occupying powers should each extract reparations from its own zone. The consequence of this decision was a *de facto* division of responsibility for the transition period. As with the settlements in other areas, temporary and transitional expedients became the basis of permanent arrangements. The Allied Control Council for Germany, riven by disputes over denazification policies, access by the occupying powers to each other's zones, and the interzonal transfer of reparations, was hardly in a position to enforce joint administration of Germany. Germany represented the European situation in microcosm. Though the United States and the Soviet Union both continued to advocate a united Germany — a policy which the Soviet Union persisted in longer than the United States — neither was willing to risk its potential cost: the absorption of Germany into the other's camp.

The atomic bomb, exploded over Hiroshima and Nagasaki by the Americans in August 1945, indoubtedly introduced a new dimension into conceptions of warfare, but its initial impact on US-Soviet relations was surprisingly limited. Revisionist historians have argued with considerable justice that the Americans hoped and believed that the demonstration of the bomb's power in bringing about the defeat of Japan would incline the Soviet Union to be more compliant in negotiations over political and territorial issues.[22] News of the first successful test of the A-bomb, which reached Truman while he was at Potsdam in late July 1945, reportedly had the effect of stiffening Truman's resolve not to yield to the Soviets on the composition of new governments in Bulgaria, Rumania, and Hungary. But to whatever degree 'atomic diplomacy' was envisaged as a means of cowing the Soviets it has to be said that it failed; the Soviet position on Eastern Europe, as John Gaddis has pointed out, 'became increasingly rigid after August 1945'.[23] The chief effect of the American test was probably to encourage the Soviet Union to step up its own nuclear program, on which it had been engaged in any case since before the war. The period of the American atomic monopoly (1945-49) were precisely those years in which atomic diplomacy might have been expected to succeed. In the event the atomic bomb proved to be a very blunt diplomatic instrument and the will to contemplate its use as a weapon of war was probably decreased by its employment against Japan.

The attempt to establish international control of nuclear power illustrates more tangibly the capacity of the nuclear issue to focus disagreements. The debate in the UN Atomic Energy Commission during the summer of 1946 on the 'Baruch Plan' was a harbinger of the nuclear arms race no less than a manifestation of the incompatibility of US and Soviet goals. Baruch's plan proposed the establishment of an international authority to oversee all phases of the development and use of atomic energy. Provision for inspection and control was integral to the plan, as was the American insistence that the United States could contemplate ending manufacture of its own weapons and disposing of its stockpile only when the machinery was in place. In response the Soviet Union called for the destruction of existing stockpiles prior to the establishment of the machinery of inspection and control. Deadlock ensued, ensuring that separate and competitive development of nuclear weapons would be the outcome.

1946: The Turning Point

In the political climate of 1946 deadlock was perhaps inevitable. Such willingness as there had been during 1945 on the part of the United States and the Soviet Union to seek common ground was fast disappearing. The crisis in Iran during March 1946 had already exposed a serious rift. Soviet delay in withdrawing troops from Iran (deployed there during the war along with British forces in order to prevent the Iranian oilfields falling into Axis hands) provoked an angry American response. Not content that the problem should be resolved by bilateral negotiations between Iran and the Soviet Union, which appeared close to success by the end of March, the United States insisted on placing the issue before the UN Security Council. In the event the Soviet Union backed down amid a flurry of resentment at the American decision to throw a public spotlight on the issue.

The decisive change during 1946 was the public acknowledgement by both sides that the Grand Alliance was moribund. Within the

United States it took the form of mounting criticism of the Truman administration's 'soft line' on Eastern Europe, focussing on Secretary of State James Byrnes who had negotiated the agreements on Bulgaria and Rumania. Byrnes himself, shifting with the times, signalled a new hard line in early February 1946 in which he acknowledged deep differences between the United States and the Soviet Union. This was followed in early March by Churchill's 'Iron Curtain' speech at Fulton, Missouri, a statement which aroused intense anger within American public opinion for its belligerent tone but which Truman and his closest advisers did little to disown. Just as telling, though still secret, was the so-called 'long telegram' from George Kennan, senior American diplomat in Moscow. This document painted a dark picture of a Soviet Union 'fanatically committed to the belief that with the US there can be no permanent *modus vivendi*, that it is desirable and necessary that the internal harmony of our society be disrupted, our traditional way of life destroyed, the international authority of our state be broken if Soviet power is to be secure.'[24] With these words Kennan uttered the as yet unspoken thoughts of the Truman administration and it brought him swiftly, though briefly as it turned out, to the centre of the policy-making process.

Kennan's assessment had been prompted by a request from the State Department for an interpretation of Soviet policy in the light of a speech by Stalin at the beginning of February. Though given as an electoral address for a domestic audience, its strident denunciation of capitalism, its picture of the war as having been the product of capitalist imperial designs, and its claim that the war proved 'that our Soviet social system has won', were hardly calculated to promote cooperation and understanding with the West.[25] It was perceived in the United States as a declaration of Cold War.

The degree to which the range of permissible views within the Truman administration was narrowing during 1946 can be gauged by the reaction to an address by Secretary of Commerce Henry Wallace given in September. 'The real peace treaty we now need is between the US and Russia', he declared, going on to suggest that, while Americans may not have liked what was going on in Eastern Europe, 'we should recognize that we have no more business in the *political* affairs of Eastern Europe than Russia has in the *political* affairs of Latin America, Western Europe, and the US'.[26] Such evenhandedness was unacceptable and Wallace was forced to resign. His error was to endorse a Soviet 'sphere of influence' in Eastern Europe. In practice the United States was left with little alternative, short of war, to accepting Soviet predominance in Eastern Europe. The situation was unpalatable, however, for a number of reasons: it left countries recently liberated from Nazi rule subject to a new form of domination and its risked alienating the large section of the American population whose ethnic roots lay in Eastern Europe. Nor were Truman and his advisers convinced that Soviet ambitions would rest with Eastern Europe. But Wallace committed the further error of equating the Soviet position in Eastern Europe with the United States' in Latin America. While, as Eduard Mark has pointed out, the Truman administration had been willing to countenance an 'open' Soviet sphere in Eastern Europe, comparable to America's benign interest in Latin America, events had dashed such hopes. The reality in Eastern Europe was Soviet domination, and Wallace's remarks seemed to Truman willfully ignorant of that fact.[27]

Wallace's enforced resignation in September 1946 registered a marked shift of mood in America. Within a month the mid-term Congressional elections had produced Republican majorities in both Houses, overthrowing a Democratic dominance of sixteen years. Into the legislature came a new cohort of Congressman, many of them war veterans (among them Richard M. Nixon and John F. Kennedy) who had learned the lesson of 'appeasement' from the war and readily transferred their hatred of Hitler's totalitarianism to Stalin's version of it. The death in January 1946 of Harry Hopkins, the embodiment of Rooseveltian aspirations for maintenance of the Grand Alliance, symbolized the passing of the wartime ethos. The exposure of a Soviet atomic spy-ring in Canada during 1946 sensitized Americans to the threat of communist subversion and within a few months of the elections Truman came under great public pressure to introduce a 'loyalty programme' for all Federal employees. These developments laid fertile ground for the subsequent activities of the House Un-American Activities Committee and of Senator Joe McCarthy, ensuring that the Cold War at home would preoccupy American public opinion as much, if not more, than the conflict abroad.

Less often noticed by historians of American policy is the fact that a similar process was taking place in the Soviet Union. The downplaying of communist ideology during the war and the elevation of Russia's national (especially military) traditions was speedily reversed after the defeat of Germany. Fearing the effects of the Soviet troops' exposure to non-communist Europe as they drove westward, Stalin quickly reinstated the Party and communist ideology as the reigning force in Soviet life. National heroes such as Marshal Zhukov, the architect of Russia's military victory, disappeared from public life within a few months of the end of the war. By 1948 *Pravda* was celebrating the third anniversary of the taking of Berlin without mentioning Zhukov.[28]

These developments raise questions about the relationship between domestic affairs and the formulation of foreign policy. Historians have had little trouble in showing that Truman strove hard to create a consensus for a hard line towards the Soviet Union, that he engaged in a vigorous campaign to discredit critics such as Wallace, and that his preference for unambiguous solutions to complex problems often served to raise the temperature of public debate.[29] As Lyndon Johnson found later in the Vietnam war, though with very different results, Truman had a war on two fronts — one with the Soviet Union and another with American public opinion which, as he saw it, needed to be persuaded of the reality of the Soviet threat. One can agree that Truman engaged in the manufacture of consent, thereby helping to promote a Cold War mentality, without, however, endorsing the view that the Soviet threat was entirely a figment of his imagination or that he was insincere in his interpretation of Soviet actions. The truth is that Truman was subject to multiple pressures: Soviet actions which he perceived to be aggressive, requests from Britain to make a commitment to the stability of Western Europe in the face of Soviet intransigence, Communist Party strength in France and Italy, and the need to justify to the American Congress and the American public an unprecedentedly active role for the United States in international affairs.

On the Soviet side too anxiety may have been triggered by American actions during the Iran crisis, by the employment of economic and atomic diplomacy, and by Churchill's Iron Curtain speech, rekindling the fear of 'encirclement' aroused during the interwar period. The result was a spiral of mutual mistrust between the powers. Stalin also had a war on the home front and he underestimated the degree to which his method of fighting it would be interpreted in the light of disagreements with the United States in the field of diplomacy. As the American Ambassador in Moscow, Walter Bedell Smith, wrote in 1949: 'The time has passed when foreign affairs and domestic affairs could be regarded as separate and distinct'.[30] Smith meant by this that the United States must gear all its domestic resources to a long struggle with the Soviet Union, but the statement has wider applications than Smith had in mind. The erosion of the boundary between foreign and domestic affairs substantially raised the stakes of diplomacy, making the Cold War a conflict of cultures no less than of nation states. '[The Cold War] has really become a matter of the defence of western civilization', wrote a British Foreign Office Official in 1948.[31] In the United States the publication of an abridgement of Arnold Toynbee's *A Study of History* (1946), a sweeping survey of the decline of great civilizations throughout world history, jangled raw American nerves. Toynbee's message that only a spiritual regeneration in the West could prevent it going the way of the Roman Empire was eagerly absorbed by an American intelligentsia seeking a counter-weight to Marxism.[32] In the end the striking feature of US-

Soviet relations in the immediate postwar years is the acute sense of vulnerability on both sides and the inability of each to comprehend the fears no less than the interests of the other.

Map No. 1
Divided Europe

III Containment and the Division of Europe, 1947-1950

Roosevelt had returned from Yalta in February 1945 declaring in his message to Congress that the agreements 'ought to spell the end of unilateral action, the exclusive alliances, the spheres of influence, the balances of power, and all the other expedients that have been tried for centuries — and have always failed'.[33] Roosevelt's hopes for a clean slate, as we have seen, were quickly undermined in the events of 1945-46, but some fluidity remained in US-Soviet relations. They were still talking to each other, trying to give tangible form to their aspirations for cooperation. In the event the outcome of these efforts was precisely those despised talismans of the bad old politics — spheres of influence, exclusive alliances and so on. . . . By 1950 they had become firmly institutionalized and management of cooperation had given way to management of conflict.

'Containment' supplied the intellectual rationale for the Truman administration's new orientation and was classically expounded by George Kennan in his article *The Sources of Soviet Conduct* (July 1947). He did not view the Soviet Union as bent upon immediate invasion of Western Europe; nor did he believe that a fanatical devotion to world-wide expansion of communism was the driving force behind Soviet policy. While Soviet ideology assumed the inevitable downfall of capitalism, no timetable was laid down by the Kremlin. The Soviets were prepared for the long haul. Given the doctrine of the infallibility of the Kremlin and the iron discipline of the Party, the Soviet leadership was 'at liberty to put forward for tactical purposes any particular thesis which it finds useful to the cause at any particular moment and require the faithful and unquestioning acceptance of that thesis by the members of the movement as a whole'. Caution and persistence characterized Soviet policy and America must respond with 'policies no less steady in their purpose, and no less variegated and resourceful in their application, than those of the Soviet Union itself'. In these circumstances the United States must seek to contain Soviet power by the 'adroit and vigilant application of counterforce at a series of constantly shifting geographical and political points'.[34]

Kennan's prescriptions for American policy appear to be unmistakably global in scope and to carry strong military implications. In fact Kennan, the supposed architect of containment, dissociated himself from many aspects of its implementation, emerging as a critic of both the Truman Doctrine and NATO. Since Kennan played such an important and ambiguous role in policy-making during these years, we can usefully employ his writings as a vantage point from which to view the institutionalization of the Cold War.

The Truman Doctrine

Containment had been enacted in the form of the Truman Doctrine before Kennan supplied the policy with a label. In March 1947 Britain announced that it could no longer afford to sustain its support for the Greek government in the civil war which raged intermittently after the liberation of Greece from the Germans in 1944. Greece had been conceded by Stalin as a Western sphere of influence in the so-called 'percentages agreement' with Churchill in October 1944. It is now clear that Stalin held to this agreement and not only withheld support to the Greek communists but was disturbed by the prospect of a communist revolution with indigenous roots. (Marshal Tito of Yugoslavia, the one communist leader in Eastern Europe not beholden to the Red Army for his position, bore out Stalin's fears when in 1948 he declared his independence from the Soviet Union.) Such distinctions, however, meant little to American leaders who could only see in the flow of arms from Yugoslavia and Albania to the Greek rebels the hand of the Soviet Union. In Turkey too, although not at risk domestically to the same degree as Greece, Soviet pressure for control of the Black Sea straits was perceived as a bid not merely for influence in Turkey but as a stepping-stone to gains in the Middle East.

The striking feature of the American response to the announcement of British withdrawal is not so much the actual decision to send economic and military aid to Greece and Turkey as the ease with which Truman was able to produce a consensus for a fundamental reorientation in American policy. Presenting a stark contrast between two alternative ways of life, 'one based upon the will of the majority' and 'one based upon the will of a minority forcibly imposed upon the majority', he declared in his speech to Congress on March 15 1947 that 'it must be the policy of the United States to support free peoples who are resisting attempted subjugation by armed minorities or by outside pressures'.[35] There seems little doubt, as historians have shown, that Truman's motive for pitching the rhetoric of his message so high was the need to convince a cost-conscious Congress and an American public opinion not yet fully congnizant of the extended role the United States was quickly assuming that the stakes were as high as he perceived them to be in Greece and Turkey. But it is equally clear that Truman and his advisors sincerely believed that the crisis was much wider than the situation in Greece and Turkey. To that extent, as Daniel Yergin has pointed out, while the message to Congress was certainly conceived as a 'sales job', it was not a cynical manoeuvre.[36]

In the congressional hearings on the Greece and Turkey Aid Bill the administration was pressed on the question of the extent of the commitment the United States was undertaking. Under-Secretary of State Dean Acheson sought to calm fears that the Truman Doctrine was a blank cheque to be drawn on at will in other comparable situations, but he barely succeeded. Each case, he said, would be considered according to the specific circumstances but he could not disguise the fact that the Truman Doctrine speech had established the framework within which such cases would be judged. This is clear in an exchange with Senator Vandenberg, a leading Republican Senator whose influence in this and other crucial policy initiatives laid the basis for bipartisan support for Truman:

> Vandenberg: . . . In other words, I think what you are saying is that wherever we find free peoples having difficulty in the maintenance of free institutions, and difficulty in defending against aggressive movements that seek to impose upon them totalitarian regimes, we do not necessarily react in the same way each time, but we propose to react.
>
> Acheson: That, I think, is correct.[37]

George Kennan objected strongly to the universalist character of the message but also to the specifics of the aid to Greece and Turkey. He opposed any aid to Turkey and felt that the emphasis in the proposals for Greece was excessively military.[38] These distinctions appear puzzling in the light of his July article already referred to. In his memoirs Kennan admits to serious deficiencies in his exposition of containment: the failure to make clear that he considered containment as primarily political and the 'failure to distinguish between various geographic areas and to make it clear that the 'containment' of which I was speaking was not something I thought we could, necessarily, do everywhere successfully'.[39] The problem seems to have arisen because Kennan's exposition in his July article was both complex and incomplete. His intention was evidently to underline the seriousness of the Soviet threat which he felt was insufficiently appreciated. In the process he overplayed his hand. Attention was thus deflected from arguably his most important suggestion that 'the issue of Soviet-American relations is in essence a test of the overall worth of the United States as a nation among nations'.[40] By extension the West's strongest card in its conflict with communism was the health and vigour of its own democratic traditions and values. This view became central to the Marshall Plan. Kennan himself has noted the irony that his name should be associated with the Truman Doctrine, about which he had serious reservations and in which he was scarcely involved, rather than the Marshall Plan, in which he was a prime, if largely unseen, mover.[41]

The Marshall Plan, Germany, and the Division of Europe, 1947-1949

The Marshall Plan was not to all appearances designed to divide Europe but such, in conjunction with other developments, was its effect. The growth of despised 'spheres of influence' was hastened by the Marshall Plan and consolidated in the division of Germany and the establishment of NATO. Once again Kennan's role is instructive. John Gaddis has drawn attention to an exchange of letters in early 1945 between Kennan and Charles Bohlen, the State Department's other leading Soviet expert. Kennan expressed the view that, given the Soviet Union's determination to dominate Eastern Europe, 'why could we not make a decent and definite compromise with it — divide Europe frankly into spheres of influence — keep ourselves out of the Russian sphere and keep the Russians out of ours?' Bohlen shared Kennan's assessment of Russian intransigence but replied that 'foreign policy of that kind cannot be made in a democracy . . . Only totalitarian states can make and carry out such policies'.[42] In the event official policy took the direction outlined by Kennan in 1945 while Kennan himself modified his stance and held out hopes for the promotion of Europe as a 'third force' independent of the superpowers. The formulation of the Marshall Plan represents the meeting point of these two trends of thought: it combines pan-European ideas with acknowledgement of the divide between East and West.

European recovery plans were already under discussion while the Truman Doctrine was being formulated. Indeed the two policies were related in the minds of the Truman administration from the start — 'two halves of the same walnut', as Truman put it. Three things provoked a reconsideration of policy towards Europe: deepening dismay at the consolidation of communist power within Eastern European governments, continuing failure to agree on a German settlement, and economic disarray in Western Europe, apparently threatening the political stability of, in particular, France and Italy.

The last presented the most urgent problem. Returning from Europe in May from a fact-finding mission, Under-Secretary of State for Economic Affairs William Clayton declared that 'it is now obvious that we grossly underestimated the destruction to the European economy by the war . . . Europe is steadily deteriorating'. The plight of Europe, however, was not his only preoccupation. In addition to the awful implications a European collapse would have for the future peace and security of the world, he wrote, 'the immediate effects on our domestic economy would be disastrous: markets for our surplus production gone, unemployment, depression, a heavily unbalanced budget on the background of a mountainous war debt. *These things must not happen*.' (sic) Concluding that the United States must therefore initiate a substantial program of aid, he remarked (with emphasis): '*The United States must run this show*'.[43]

Clayton represented the hard-nosed side of the Marshall Plan, its economic bottom line. The State Department's Policy Planning Staff (PPS), headed by George Kennan, was less bald in its perception of the consequences for the US economy of European decline, and emphasized rather the goal of restoring Europe's faith in its future. In a document which was heavily drawn on by Marshall in his public announcement of the European Recovery Program (ERP) in June, Kennan was at pains to stress that 'the American effort in aid to Europe should be directed not to the combatting of communism but to the restoration of the economic health and vigour of European society'. He insisted also that the initiative must come from Europe and must be jointly conceived by all participating countries.[44] The conception was thus of a plan which would promote European unity as well as economic revival, with the overall aim of creating a stable and independent European bloc.

But how much of Europe? The PPS addressed itself primarily to Western Europe but also felt it necessary to consider the possibility of Soviet and East European participation. The way in which Soviet bloc participation was discussed, however, shows that it was neither genuinely desired nor really anticipated. It was essential, Kennan believed, that the proposal for general European cooperation 'be done in such a form that the Russian satellite countries would either exclude themselves by unwillingness to accept the proposed conditions or agree to abandon the exclusive orientation of their economies'.[45] Not surprisingly, the Soviet Union was unwilling to accede to conditions which would involve opening its economy to Western penetration. Having accepted the invitation to attend the opening ERP meeting in Paris, the Soviet representative withdrew, once the conditions had been made explicit, and placed pressure on the Poles and Czechs to follow suit.

The announcement of the Marshall Plan had implications for the whole range of European issues which divided the United States and the Soviet Union. The Soviet response was swift and unequivocal. Four days after his return from Paris, Foreign Secretary Molotov announced the establishment of the Communist Information Bureau (Cominform), designed to strengthen Soviet control in Eastern Europe. In Hungary non-communists within the government were purged and Cominform leader, Andre Zhdanov, embarked on a campaign of ideological vilification of the West which included a call to French and Italian Communists to foment disruption and seek the elimination of all non-communist leftists in their countries. Whether one interprets these actions as a defensive response to a perceived threat of Western encroachment on Eastern Europe or as an aggressive design for the destabilization of Western Europe makes little difference to the essential point: that the Marshall Plan forced Stalin to reassses his stance towards Europe East and West.[46] The communist coup in Czechoslovakia in February 1948 was the most dramatic outcome of this process, removing the only remaining non-communist leader in Eastern Europe. Since 1945 President Benes had trodden a careful path between remaining on good terms with the Soviets and resisting communist control. The fall of his government under the pressure of Soviet troops stationed on the Czech border, coupled with the suicide of his Foreign Minister Jan Masaryck under suspicious circumstances, profoundly shocked the West. Its immediate effect within the United States was to hasten the vote on appropriations for the Marshall Plan which had languished in Congress for eight months. Amidst a war scare Truman went before Congress to impress upon legislators that the survival of freedom was at stake.

The German issue too was inseparable from the Marshall Plan. In January 1947 the British and American zones had been formally merged, an acknowledgement that four-power control of Germany was not working and was unlikely to work. American policy was now aimed frankly at rebuilding the West German economy. An important goal of the Marshall Plan was to calm French fears about a revived Germany by integrating West Germany into a Europe-wide system. German recovery, the Americans argued, was vital to the economic health of Europe. Two important steps were then taken at a conference of the United States and five West European nations held in London in February 1948: the decision to introduce a new currency into West Germany to provide financial stability for economic revival and an as yet tentative move towards West German statehood. Again France's anxieties were aroused about German revanchism and were soothed in this instance by an American commitment to retain some troops indefinitely in Europe. Though aimed at containing Germany rather than the Soviet Union this decision coincided with discussion on the establishment of NATO. The militarization of containment flowed inexorably from the logic supplied by the economic and political decisions of 1947-48.

The Soviet reaction to the introduction of the new currency in West Germany (including West Berlin) ensured that this logic would be played out. The day after the new Deutschmark was introduced the Soviets cut the land routes between West Germany and West Berlin. The Berlin blockade began on June 24 1948 and lasted for nearly a year until the airlift mounted by the United States and Britain convinced the Soviet Union that the only alternative to accepting the 'illogic' of a Western enclave deep within the Soviet zone was war.

Indeed at no time since the end of hostilities in 1945 had war seemed so likely. While the blockade stretched out, as Louis Halle has observed, 'sixty long-range bombers of the US airforce were quietly moved across the Atlantic to the British Isles', to remain there and be reinforced subsequently.[47] The German (though not the Berlin) problem was 'solved' by the adoption in May 1949 of a constitution which established the Federal Republic of Germany (FRG). The Soviet Union responded immediately with the formation of the German Democratic Republic (GDR).

NATO, NSC-68 and the Militarization of Containment

Daniel Yergin has identified the growth of a 'national security state' in the postwar decade — the organization of the United States 'for perpetual confrontation and for war'.[48] At a time in mid-1946 when the United States was demobilizing fast, Truman's Special Counsel, Clark Clifford, wrote to the President that 'in restraining the Soviet Union the United States must be prepared to wage atomic and biological warfare. A highly mechanized army, which can be moved either by sea or by air, capable of seizing and holding strategic areas, must be supported by powerful naval and air forces'.[49] A year later a new Defense Act created a more integrated defence organization, including a single Department of Defense to replace the separately run armed services, and a National Security Council to advise the President on the whole range of defence activities. War plans in the event of conflict with the Soviet Union were being formulated as Europe fractured down the line of the Iron Curtain.

As yet, however, there was no consensus within Congress, to say nothing of the country at large, on the desirability or need for an extensive US military commitment to the defence of Western Europe. Many of those Senators and Congressman who were loudest in their demands for a tough line against the Soviet Union were precisely those who resisted granting appropriations for military purposes. The debate in Congress on NATO itself reflected the strength of these feelings. While there was a good measure of agreement on the need for American participation in some form of security pact with Western European nations, there was little appetite for a large US force permanently stationed in Europe. When asked whether the administration planned to send 'substantial' numbers of US troops to shore up the European defences, Acheson assured the Senate [that] 'the answer to that question . . . is a clear and absolute no'.[50] The Senate was similarly assured that there was no plan for the rearmament of Germany. The NATO pact was conceived by the administration, or at least presented publicly, as a confidence booster to Europe to prevent it succumbing politically to appeasement or neutrality under Soviet pressure.

A marked change in the conception of NATO was produced by the detection in September 1949 of a Soviet atom bomb test. The Truman administration had convinced itself, against the views of American atomic scientists, that the Soviet Union would take twenty years to manufacture its own bomb. News of the Soviet test threw these calculations to the winds, setting off a frantic search for the traitors who had passed the secret of the bomb to the Soviets. In Klaus Fuchs (captured and found guilty by the British in March 1950) and the Rosenbergs (also convicted in early 1950) such traitors were found, though it is possible that the Soviet atomic program would have achieved its end with little delay in the absence of espionage.[51] The military and strategic implications of the ending of the American atomic monopoly, however, profoundly affected the calculations of American policy-makers. In conjunction with the 'loss' of China in 1949 and the beginnings of Joseph McCarthy's attacks on the Truman administration's weak response to communism, news of the Soviet test produced pressure for a fundamental reassessment of America's strategic objectives and plans. It took the form of a lengthy document, justifiably considered by historians as equal in significance to the Truman Doctrine speech, known as National Security Council Resolution 68 (NSC-68).

NSC-68 illustrates the inseparability of military and ideological concerns in this critical year of the Cold War. The challenge presented by the Soviet Union was conceived to be moral as much as material. With the eclipse of freedom in Czechoslovakia two years before, 'it was in the intangible scale of values that we registered a loss more damaging than the material loss we had already suffered'. However, in order to convince the Soviet Union of its determination to uphold the idea of freedom ('the most contagious idea in history'), the United States must match its capabilities to its intentions. 'Without superior aggregate military strength, in being and readily mobilizable, a policy of 'containment' — which is in effect a policy of calculated and gradual coercion — is no more than a policy of bluff'.[52] The result was the decision to embark upon a rapid build-up of political, economic, and military strength in the Free World.

NSC-68 was commissioned by Truman in January 1950, forwarded to the President in April, and approved in September. Of central importance in converting the document from a blueprint for a massive arms build-up into practical policy was the outbreak of the Korean War in June of the same year. (This is discussed in section IV). There is no need to claim US complicity in bringing about the North Korean attack, as some historians have argued, to recognize that the beginning of the Korean war confirmed the logic of NSC-68 and eased its implementation. By the time the Korean War ended in 1953 the United States had substantially bolstered its forces in Western Europe and begun the delicate task of promoting the rearmament of West Germany.[53] Above all, NSC-68 was explicitly global in scope and military in application. Negotiation was not abandoned as a goal but remained carefully circumscribed by military priorities. As the authors of NSC-68 put it, 'negotiation is not a separate course of action but rather a means of gaining support for a program of building strength, of recording, where necessary and desirable, progress in the cold war . . .'[54] In short, Kennan's beliefs in the need for selectivity in American commitments, for the primacy of the political over the military, and for a policy based on Soviet intentions rather than capabilities were firmly sidelined with the adoption of NSC-68.

NSC-68 established the framework of American policy for the next twenty years. It might be described as 'containment-plus' in that it anticipates John Foster Dulles's policies of 'liberation' and 'rollback', announced in the early 1950s. It was not, however, wholly lacking in flexibility. Recording 'progress in the cold war' was a vague formula which allowed for strategic retreats from exposed positions. Despite, for example, the verbal support given to the Hungarian reformers of 1956, the United States clearly had no intention of backing words with actions to the extent of risking war with the Soviet Union. As the tanks rolled into Budapest to crush the rebellion, American policy-makers wrung their hands but did little more. Where, however, the United States felt that its interests could be advanced at acceptable cost, then NSC-68 proved capacious enough to accommodate them. In the Far East the costs proved if anything greater than in Europe. To this we now turn.

IV Cold War in the Far East

McCarthyism and the Far Eastern Turn

Truman was politically vulnerable in the early months of 1950. The twin blows of the Soviet atom test and the Chinese Revolution had shaken public confidence in the administration's policies, exposing it to charges of negligence and worse. The conviction of Alger Hiss for perjury in January 1950 seemed to confirm suspicions that the Truman and Roosevelt administrations had harboured traitors in key policy-making positions. Hiss had worked in the State Department during the late 1930s, had been a member of the American delegation at Yalta, and after the war had been appointed President of the Carnegie

Endowment for International Peace. The specific charge against him was that he had perjured himself before the House Un-American Activities Committee in denying that he had passed information to the Russians while employed at the State Department in 1937-38. (Thanks to the Statute of Limitations, he could not be charged with espionage as such.) In actuality Hiss's role in policy-making had been a minor one, but the case became a convenient peg on which critics of the Truman administration could hang a series of accusations, amounting to a comprehensive denunciation of the whole Roosevelt-Truman record in foreign policy.

For figures such as Senator Joseph McCarthy, who rose to prominence in the wake of the Hiss conviction, the case provided an explanation for the succession of American defeats in the Cold War, beginning with the 'sell-out' of Eastern Europe to the Soviets at Yalta and culminating in the 'loss' of China. No note is more consistently sounded in McCarthy's speeches than his belief in America's 'impotency' in the face of communism, 'the feeling of America's weakness in the very air we breathe in Washington'. The present situation could only be accounted for as the product of 'a great conspiracy, a conspiracy on a scale so immense as to dwarf any previous such venture in the history of man'. Hiss's cultured, urbane demeanour, his association with the east coast liberal élite, and his deep roots in Roosevelt's New Deal offered easy targets for Republican vilification of the betrayers of true Americanism and heralded the end of bipartisanship on foreign policy within Congress. Dean Acheson, Marshall's successor as Secretary of State, blackened the Democrats' record still further when he announced, following the conviction of his old friend, that 'I will not turn my back on Alger Hiss'. With this statement, said McCarthy, 'this pompous diplomat in striped pants, with a phony British accent . . . awakened the dormant indignation of the American people'.[55] For four years McCarthy pressed home his message, throwing the administration on to the defensive and ensuring that the communist issue would dictate the agenda of domestic affairs.

McCarthy did not invent anti-communism. His genius was to dramatize the issue, to put his personal imprint upon it by a combination of adroit self-publicity and unscrupulous exploitation of the media's appetite for sensational copy. His targets were many — the State department, the Democratic Party, and subsequently the army and the Presidency. By 1954 he had become an embarrassment to his own party. Republicans who had been content to go along with McCarthy's attacks on the Democrats, especially for their conduct of the Korean War, balked at his increasingly indiscriminate charges against such hallowed institutions as the army and the (now Republican) presidency. In 1954 he was censured by the Senate and effectively silenced. Within three years he was dead, a broken man mired in alcoholism.

There are many contexts in which McCarthy and McCarthyism can be viewed. A rich literature on the political and sociological roots of the American anxiety about communism began to appear within months of McCarthy's censure by the Senate.[56] From the standpoint of foreign relations, however, the significance of McCarthy's career lies in the coincidence of his brief period of notoriety with the shift of attention from Europe to the Far East, a shift which he helped to promote. Two figures appear repeatedly in his catalogue of traitors —George Marshall and Owen Lattimore. Both, it was claimed, had been instrumental in the disastrous policy of denying adequate support to the Chinese Nationalists under Chiang Kai-Shek, hence paving the way for the Communist victory of 1949. The Korean War, and Chinese entry on the side of North Korea, would never have happened, it was argued, if the Truman administration had given due attention to the danger of communism in the Far East rather than devoting its resources to Europe in the crucial years after 1945.

Once again, McCarthy was not the initiator of the 'Asia first' view. Its roots lay in controversy over the United States' wartime 'Europe-first' strategy and gained powerful advocates within Congress and among prominent publishers and businessman in the immediate postwar years. Henry Luce, publisher of *Time* and *Life*, was a persistent supporter of the Chinese Nationalists and critic of the Truman policy of seeking to resolve the civil war in China by bringing the Nationalists and Communists together. Madame Chiang, a Christian with close ties to American businessmen and legislators, lobbied energetically on behalf of the Nationalist cause both before and after the Revolution. Within Congress Senator Knowland's role in this cause was such that, following the Nationalists' flight to Formosa (Taiwan), he was dubbed 'the Senator from Formosa'. The links which the Asia firsters and the China Lobby managed to forge between the communist threat in Asia and inside America had profound effects upon the future of America's involvement in the Far East. It ensured that recognition of Communist China would remain off the agenda for a long time to come. It removed from office the cream of America's China specialists in the State Department purge which followed the Chinese revolution.[57] It also encouraged a heightened sensitivity to the dangers of further losses to communism in Asia. Thereafter, compromise or accommodation with Asian communism was tantamount to abject surrender.

China, Japan, and the Ferment in Asia, 1945-1950

The Asia firsters' contention that the Truman administration had lost China is justified only if one accepts their premises that China was

America's to lose. This view was based on the romantic notion that the United States had a record of benign concern for China, stemming from the 'Open Door' notes of 1899. In opposing the European nations' plans to parcel up China in line with their own economic interests, the United States, it was felt, had demonstrated an enlightened concern for China's territorial integrity. While extensive cultural and educational ties existed between China and the United States, in fact the United States did little to enforce the principle of the open door, which in any case could be seen as a self-interested claim for an economic stake by a latecomer on the Chinese scene. In other spheres too China had little reason to feel beholden to the United States. Discriminatory American immigration laws and maltreatment of the Chinese population within the United States were a constant source of friction from the 1880s onwards. Nor did successive American administrations do much to aid China in the face of Japan's growing aspirations to dominance in the Far East. With the (admittedly reluctant) support of the United States, Japan gained concessions in the Shantung Peninsula at China's expense at the Treaty of Versailles (1919); the Japanese invasion of Manchuria in 1931 produced only verbal protests from the United States; and when full-scale war broke out between China and Japan in 1937 Roosevelt shrank from imposing sanctions on Japan.

American policy towards China changed substantially with the deterioration of American-Japanese relations in 1940-41. Indeed the cause of this deterioration was increasing encroachment by Japan on China as well as South East Asia. In this sense the United States 'special relationship' with China was a late development; too late, it might be said, given that China was burdened with internal disruption in addition to the war with Japan. Having once made the decision to support China with lend-lease and to build up China as a major power by including her in the councils of the anti-Axis nations, the United States was confronted by the problem of supporting a leader — Chiang Kai-shek — whose hold on power was distinctly fragile. The central issue for American policy-makers in the wartime and immediate postwar years was their attitude towards the relations between the Chinese Nationalists and the Communists.

Contradictory advice was reaching Washington from China as the war drew to a close. Ambassador Hurley (appointed in January 1945) advocated unreserved support for Chiang in his drive against the Communists, while counsellors within his Embassy doubted Chiang's ability to produce stable government and were critical of his dictatorial style. Ironically, McCarthy's bête noire, Owen Lattimore, held a more favourable view of Chiang than many other old 'China hands', perhaps because he had worked as Chiang's political adviser during the war. In a widely read book published in 1945 Lattimore wrote that Chiang was not at present 'losing control'. Nevertheless he felt that there was a case for political compromise with the Communists. The Communists, he wrote, 'have done well enough in the territory they control to stand comparison with the Kuomintang [Nationalists]'.[58] Hurley was incensed at the signs that Washington was leaning towards a policy of seeking to reconcile the Nationalists and Communists and on November 26 1945 he resigned in protest. 'It is no secret', he wrote in his letter of resignation to Truman, 'that the professional foreign service men sided with the Chinese Communist armed party . . . Our professional diplomats continuously advised the Communists that my efforts in preventing a collapse of the National Government did not represent the policy of the United States'.[59]

In truth Hurley's view did not fully represent the policy of the United States Government. Truman's policy was signalled in late 1945 by his dispatch of General Marshall to China to bring about a cease-fire between the Nationalists and Communists and to encourage the formation of a coalition government. After a year of largely fruitless attempts to mediate between the rival factions, Marshall returned empty-handed. (Marshall subsequently paid dearly for his efforts at the hand of McCarthy, who in 1951 launched a 60,000 word diatribe against him in Congress, later published as a book.)[60] By 1947 the United States resolved on a course of recognition of the Nationalist government, coupled with moderate economic and military aid. As the civil war raged and the Communists advanced, aid to China was gradually scaled down and in January 1949 the American Military Advisory Group was withdrawn. As Foster Rhea Dulles has pointed out, the climax of the civil war coincided with the Berlin Blockade and the prospect of a Communist victory in China did not seem to weigh heavily enough to warrant a large allocation of military resources.[61]

By the early months of 1949, as a Communist victory approached, angry Republicans produced a 'round robin' letter in Congress accusing Acheson of 'irresponsibility' in his China policy, and followed it up by introducing a series of China aid bills in Congress with the aim of pressuring the administration into action. These efforts achieved partial success, since the administration needed Congressional support for continuance of aid to Europe under the Marshall Plan. A moderate package of assistance to Chiang was passed as an amendment to a European aid bill. It would appear, however, that by the middle of the year the administration was more or less reconciled to a Communist victory in China and was bracing itself for the inevitable reaction within the United States. In August the State Department published the *China White Paper*, a lengthy history and justification of American policy accompanied by extensive documentary evidence. In the appended Letter of Transmittal from Acheson to Truman it was argued, to the consternation of the administration's critics, that 'the ominous result of the civil war in China was beyond the control of the government of the United States'.[62] That this was no more nor less than the truth did not mollify Truman's opponents, who believed that his policy of heavily qualified support for Chiang had been a self-fulfilling prophecy. A new set of battle lines was thus drawn around the related questions of recognition of Mao's China and the United States's attitude towards the Nationalist regime which at the end of the year fled to the island of Formosa.

Non-recognition of Mao and unequivocal support for Chiang was by no means a foregone conclusion. For one thing, this policy would incur the risk of war in support of Chiang and neither Truman nor the Joint Chiefs of Staff favoured such a course. A strong lobby within the State Department argued for a 'realistic' policy of recognizing whoever was fully in control. (Britain recognized Mao's government in 1950.) The scales were tipped away from Truman's preference for disengagement from the China conflict by the influence of McCarthy and the Asia firsters, as we have seen, but more decisively by the outbreak of the Korean War in June 1950 and China's entry on the side of North Korea in October. The Korean War settled another important question which had been hanging fire for a number of years — the signing of a peace treaty with Japan. Before discussing the Korean War we must consider briefly the development of policy towards Japan.

In many respects Japan's place in American Asian policy parallels that of Germany in Europe. Early designs for a punitive settlement were quickly shelved as it became clear that communism was on the march in Asia. Initially the reconstruction of Japan was premised on the need to remove the entrenched elites and institutions which had given rise to militarism in the 1930s. Democratization of the political system, dismemberment of the family-based industrial monopolies (or *zaibatsu*), and the elimination of Japan's capacity to produce heavy industrial goods (including, of course, war material) were all aimed at uprooting authoritarianism and encouraging a wider distribution of wealth and political power. To a degree each of these policies was embarked upon but, as Michael Schaller has observed, they gradually 'lost momentum or changed direction in 1948'.[63] The *zaibatsu* essentially survived efforts to break them up and the new constitution, while establishing formal democracy and liberal principles, allowed ruling conservatives to retain their position. The plan to deindustrialize Japan was never realized since it soon became clear, as was the case in Germany, that a weak and unstable Japan would invite communist inroads and would undermine America's broader goal of setting up a counter-weight to communism in Asia.[64] The change of policy towards Japan coincided with the mounting of the Marshall Plan and the Truman Doctrine in Europe. Japan became the keystone of containment in Asia.

The development of the occupation policy in Japan bears directly on the administration's reluctance to get involved too deeply in the internal affairs of China. The United States were able to exert control over the Japanese situation to an extent which they were not able to do in China. Indeed the United States insisted from the outset that the Soviet Union should have only a nominal role in the occupation of Japan, a point which the Soviets exploited to the full in their claim for a similar role in the Balkans and Eastern Europe.[65] Though it is going too far to say that the administration viewed China as expendable, it is the case that Japan was increasingly regarded as the strategic key to the American position in Asia. From the evidence of PPS and NSC documents in 1948-49, policy was formulated in anticipation of the fall of the Nationalist regime and the recurring theme is the danger of an extensive commitment to preventing its defeat.[66] When in January 1950 Dean Acheson announced the 'defensive perimeter' which the United States must be prepared to defend in Asia, it excluded not only Formosa but also Korea. America's policy in Asia was an offshore policy, reflecting the prevailing conventional wisdom that the United States should resist being drawn into a land war in Asia. In the event the North Korean attack not only undermined this policy, it also removed any remaining obstacles to the formalization of America's relations with Japan. Ironically, as Schaller points out, the North Korean attack 'set the stage for the termination of the Occupation'.[67] Any qualms about reaching a separate peace with Japan were now brushed aside. Though the Treaty was signed amid the trappings of an international conference in San Francisco in September 1951 (which the Soviet Union also attended), its provisions — which included a security pact and the granting of American forces base rights — reflected exclusively bilateral interests between the United States and Japan. The Soviet Union refused to sign.

The Korean War

The Truman administration showed little hesitation in revising its assumptions about involvement in a land war in Asia. Within a few days of the North Korean attack on June 25, 1950 it had committed ground troops to the defence of South Korea, pushed a resolution through the UN labelling North Korea as the aggressor, and interposed the 7th Fleet between Formosa and the mainland to prevent an attack by the People's Republic of China. Militarily the course of the war fluctuated wildly in the first few months. The initial push by the North Koreans took them deep into the South by the

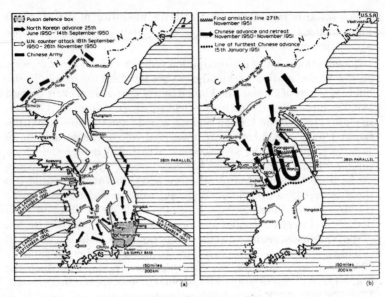

Map No. 2 (a) & Map No. 2 (b)
The Korean War, First and Second Phases

middle of September and left only a corner of the peninsula beyond their reach. General MacArthur, seconded from his post as occupation commander in Japan, responded with an outflanking amphibious attack at Inchon, a port half way up the west coast, and within a month had retaken Seoul and driven the North Koreans back to the line dividing North and South Korea at the 38th parallel. MacArthur's military success raised the question of America's political aims in Korea — to reestablish the *status quo* or to revise it by reunifying Korea?

The division of Korea had followed the pattern of Germany since 1945 — provisional partition following the removal of the Japanese wartime occupation forces, failure of the United States and the Soviet Union to agree on a means of reunification, and the establishment of separate governments in North and South. The initial UN resolution on the Korean War envisaged only the restoration of the 38th parallel but the success of MacArthur's northward drive held out the inviting prospect of reunification by force of arms. Containment, it appeared, was giving way to 'roll-back' as Truman endorsed military operations north of the 38th parallel and gained UN approval for it. Ignoring China's warnings that they would intervene if the Americans continued north, MacArthur pushed deep into the North, reaching the North Korean border with China at the Yalu river at the end of

October. As promised, the Chinese entered the war and by the end of the year had forced the UN forces into a headlong retreat down the peninsula to a point south of the 38th parallel.

Truman's response was a combination of strident verbal aggression against China — including a hint that the United States reserved the option of using the atomic bomb — and a strategic retreat to the initial goal of restoring the 38th parallel. The signs he was giving at the end of 1950 and the beginning of 1951, however, were sufficiently confused to arouse dismay in a variety of quarters. The British Prime Minister, Attlee, rushed to Washington in early December to express his anxiety about the direction of American policy. In a series of conversations with Truman Attlee urged him to open negotiations with the Chinese in order to avoid the possibility of an all-out war with China. Though no more was heard publicly about using atomic bombs in Korea, Attlee failed to convince Truman and Acheson that a less belligerent policy towards China might cool the situation in Korea and also encourage a split between Peking and Moscow. The United States was by now too committed to Chiang and to the view that accommodation to the committee in one sphere meant capitulation everywhere to find Attlee's arguments acceptable.

In practice, however, Truman was as concerned as Attlee to avoid war with China. Without conceding Attlee's point about the possible advantages for policy in Asia in general of negotiating with China, he acknowledged the narrower point about the danger of an all-out war. A serious obstacle in the way of this policy was General MacArthur, whose bellicose pronouncements and evident desire to extend the war into China became a serious embarrassment to Truman. Though it could be said that MacArthur was simply following through the logic of the decision to press forward north of the 38th parallel, after the Chinese entry the costs of that policy looked to Truman to be excessive. By April 1951, with MacArthur now back at the 38th parallel, eager to cross it once again into the North, and demanding unconditional surrender from the Chinese, Truman ordered his recall. Containment was re-established as the reigning orthodoxy.

Having escaped one set of costs, however, by ruling out war with China, Truman then incurred another — the storm of protests within the United States which greeted his dismissal of MacArthur. MacArthur returned to the United States as a conquering hero denied his booty, to be fêted by Congress and public opinion. Whether these protesters would really have welcomed war with China is open to question. It was enough that MacArthur offered a sounding board for public frustration at the conduct of the war. As the front stabilised around the 38th parallel, military stalemate ensued, though at enormous cost in casualties. It was two years before negotiations, continually stalled over the issue of the return of prisoners of war, brought a conclusion to the conflict.

Korea has been described as a 'limited war', an exemplary case of containment in action. But, as we have seen, it also illustrates the fine line in American policy between containment and rollback. The words used by Walter Lippmann to characterise Soviet intentions in the Cold War seem to apply equally well to the United States in the case of Korea: 'They will expand the revolution, if the balance of power is such that they can; if it is such that they cannot, they will make the best settlement they can obtain for Russia and the regime in Russia'.[68] The best the Americans could obtain in Korea was a return to the lines which existed in 1950. It was not in all respects, however, a return to the *status quo ante*, since it was associated with a deepened commitment to holding the line in Asia generally. The geostrategic and ideological assumptions which had led to the original formulation of containment in Europe were now firmly adopted in Asia. These included the 'domino theory' — that a loss of one country to communism would set up a chain reaction in its neighbours — and the belief that by whatever devious route all manifestations of communism were to be traced to the activities of the Kremlin.

The situations in Europe and Asia, however, were very different. The United States had little control over the course of events in Eastern Europe, largely because of the presence of the Red Army. In Asia, the challenge of communism was more complex. Connections between Soviet communism and its indigenous forms in Asia certainly existed but Asian communism was never simply the creature of the Soviet Union as was the case in Eastern Europe. If it had been — if the Soviet Union had viewed, say, Indochina as equally vital to its security as Poland — then the Vietnam War would quickly have become a world war. In fact the Soviet Union was cautious in its support for Vietnam's Ho Chi Minh in the early stages of his drive for Vietnam's independence (1945-1950) as it was decisive in its control over Poland. By a curious irony the United States was powerless to liberate Eastern Europe from communism where it had been imposed by force of arms but harboured the belief that communism could be defeated in Asia where it had indigenous roots. In Europe the reality principle operated, frustrating as it was. In Asia no such check existed, or only intermittently, and it took defeat in Vietnam to bring the lesson home.

V Conclusion

It is easy to assume that all the dilemmas faced by American policymakers in the postwar decade arose from the relationship with the Soviet Union. In fact the United States would have taken on an expanded role in world politics and in the international economy if the Soviet Union had not existed. The destruction of Europe saw to that. The United States was simply assuming the role which matched its economic and military power, as demonstrated in the war. Even then its adoption of an extended 'peacetime' role was marked by indecision and confusion in the initial stages. The desire to demobilize quickly, to renew civilian occupations, to 'return to normalcy', account in part for this, and isolationist or non-interventionist sentiment remained strong. Interventionism was also the result of pressure from Britain and Western Europe to step into the Great Power breach which they could no longer fill. As has often been pointed out, the chief antagonist of the Soviet Union among the Western powers immediately after the war was Britain, not the United States. The United States initially saw its role, as Roosevelt had during the war, as that of mediator between Britain and the Soviet Union.

Once the decision was made in 1947 to engage in containment of Soviet power, however, the United States embraced the role with a firmness and fervour which owed much to ideological conflict with the Soviet Union and helped to further it. There is an instructive analogy with American intervention in the First World War. Entry into the war in 1917 followed upon a period of uneasy neutrality during which in practice if not in theory the United States favoured the Allies against Germany. Once in the war, a political and emotional climate resulted which was repeated after the Cold War began — the emergence of a wartime psychology, pressure for ideological conformity, the characterization of the enemy as devil, and the justification of a new diplomacy in universalist terms. In this sense the American Cold War experience was firmly within the nation's traditions. The key difference was that thirty years on from 1917 there was no safe haven of normalcy to return to.

The Soviet Union's problems too in the early postwar years cannot be summed up in its relations with the United States. Economic reconstruction and security were its chief concerns, but these quickly involved the exertion of political authority in neighbouring states whose cultural ties lay with the West and who had a legacy of mistrust of Russia.[69] Then as now Soviet energies have been deployed to a considerable degree in maintaining control within its own sphere. Soviet actions in the early Cold War were thus a consequence of weakness rather than strength — or rather, economic weakness compensated for by military power and the imposition of political conformity in its 'buffer zone' with the West. In this sense the Soviet Union's creation of a sphere of influence was as much a product of the war as was the United States' economic supremacy.

If, as has been justifiably claimed, postwar US-Soviet relations constitute a Cold War 'system',[70] it is one which has been characterized by asymmetries rather than parallelisms. America's superior economic power was not of itself sufficient to assure the stability of Western Europe and it was quickly supplemented by the NATO Alliance. Even so, the geopolitical and military mismatch between the Soviet Union and the United States — Soviet ground troop superiority in Europe against US reliance on air power and nuclear weapons — remained a potent source of friction between the powers and of frustration within the United States. The United States was and is confronted with a strategic dilemma — the possibility of a Soviet invasion of Western Europe with conventional forces in the event of which the United States feels it has to reserve the option of a nuclear response. The search for security, however, has bred further insecurity, as the history of the arms race shows. In every field of policy ambitions are matched by constraints. The origins of the Cold War are to be found as much in these constraints and the attempt by both sides to surmount them as in the dictates of ideology.

NOTES

1. See Stephen Cohen, *Rethinking the Soviet Experience: Politics and History Since 1917* (New York: Oxford University Press, 1985).

2. Zbigniew Brzezinski, 'Communist Ideology: Key to Soviet Thinking', in Norman A. Graebner, ed., *The Cold War: A Conflict of Ideology And Power* (Lexington, Mass: D. C. Heath, 1976), pp.79-96.

3. John Spanier, *American Foreign Policy Since World War II* (New York: Praeger, 1960), p.16; George F. Kennan, *American Diplomacy, 1900-1950* (Chicago: University of Chicago Press, 1951), p.93.

4. Walter Lippmann to Arthur Schlesinger Jr, September 25 1967 in John Morton Blum, ed., *Public Philosopher: The Selected Letters of Walter Lippmann* (New York: Ticknor and Fields, 1985), p.615-16.

5. William Appleman Williams, *The Tragedy of American Diplomacy* (Second revised and enlarged edition, New York: Delta, 1972); Gabriel Kolko *The Politics of War: Allied Diplomacy and the World Crisis 1943-45* (London: Weidenfeld and Nicolson, 1969) and Joyce and Gabriel Kolko, *The Limits of Power: The World and United States Foreign Policy, 1945-1954* (New York: Harper and Row, 1972).

6. See David Horowitz, *From Yalta to Vietnam* (Harmondsworth: Penguin, 1967).

7. See Thomas McCormick, 'Drift or Mastery: A Corporatist Synthesis for American Diplomatic History', *Reviews in American History* 10 (December 1982), pp.318-330.

8. See John Lewis Gaddis, *The United States and the Origins of the Cold War, 1941-1947* (New York: Columbia University Press), pp.359-61.

9. Daniel Yergin, *Shattered Peace: The Origins of the Cold War and the American National Security State* (Harmondsworth: Penguin, 1980).

10. See specially Roy Douglas, *From War to Cold War: 1942-1948* (London: Macmillan, 1980); Victor Rothwell, *Britain and the Cold War, 1941-1947* (London: Cape, 1982); Terry Anderson, *The United States, Great Britain, and the Cold War, 1941-1947* (Columbia: University of Missouri Press, 1981); Fraser J. Harbutt, *The Iron Curtain: Churchill, America and the Origins of the Cold War* (New York: Oxford University Press, 1986); and Henry Butterfield Ryan, *The Vision of Anglo-America: The US-UK Alliance and the Emerging Cold War, 1943-1946* (Cambridge: Cambridge University Press, 1987).

11. Gaddis, *The United States and the Origins of the Cold War*, p.vii.

12. Quoted in John Foster Dulles, 'To Save Humanity from the Deep Abyss', *New York Times Magazine,* July 30, 1950, p.35.

13. Spanier, *American Foreign Policy Since World War II*, ch. 1; and Bruce Kuniholm, 'The Origins of the First Cold War', in Richard Crockatt and Steve Smith, ed., *The Cold War Past and Present* (London: Allen and Unwin, 1987), pp.51-54.

14. Louis Hartz, *The Liberal Tradition in America* (New York: Harcourt Brace, 1955), Ch. I.

15. Geoffrey Barraclough, *An Introduction to Contemporary History* (Harmondsworth: Penguin, 1967), p.120, 118.

16. Vojtech Mastny has shown, however, that dissolution of the Comintern has other motives. Stalin had found the Comintern an unserviceable means of controlling non-Soviet Communist parties and believed that he could more easily achieve his purposes by dealing with them individually. See *Russia's Road to the Cold War: Diplomacy, Warfare and the Politics of Communism, 1941-1945* (New York: Columbia University Press, 1979), pp.95-7.

17. Milovan Djilas, *Conversations with Stalin* (New York: Harcourt Brace, 1962), p.114.

18. Quoted in Robert A. Pollard, *Economic Security and the Origins of the Cold War, 1945-1950* (New York: Columbia University Press, 1985), p.8.

19. Gaddis, *The United States and the Origins of the Cold War*, p.23.

20. Quoted in Mastny, *Russia's Road to the Cold War*, p.218.

21. See Gaddis, *The United States and the Origins of the Cold War*, pp.238-41.

22. See especially Gar Alperovitz, *Atomic Diplomacy: Hiroshima, Potsdam. The Use of the Atomic Bomb and the Confrontation with the Soviet Union* (Revised edition, New York: Penguin, 1985).

23. Gaddis, *The United States and the Origins of the Cold War*, p.246.

24. George F. Kennan's 'long telegram' in Joseph M. Siracusa, ed., *The American Diplomatic Revolution: A Documentary History of the Cold War* (Milton Keynes: Open University Press, 1976), p.195. The speeches by Byrnes and Churchill are printed in the same volume, pp.201-6 and 206-9.

25. In Siracusa, ed., *The American Diplomatic Revolution*, p.180.

26. In Siracusa, ed., *The American Diplomatic Revolution*, p.210.

27. On the question of the distinction between 'open' and 'exclusive' spheres of influence see Eduard Marks, 'American Policy Toward Eastern Europe and the Origins of the Cold War: An Alternative Interpretation', *Journal of American History* **68** (1981-82), pp.313-336.

28. See Isaac Deutscher, *Stalin: A Political Biography* (New York: Vintage, 1960), pp.555-565.

29. See, for example, Thomas A. Paterson, *Meeting the Communist Threat: Truman to Reagan* (New York: Oxford University Press, 1988), Chs. 1-3, 5 and 6.

30. Walter Bedell Smith, *Moscow Mission, 1946-1949* (London: Heinemann, 1950), p.327.

31. John Lewis Gaddis, *The Long Peace: Inquiries into the History of the Cold War* (New York: Oxford University Press, 1987), p.46.

32. Arnold J. Toynbee, *A Study of History* (New York: Oxford University Press, 1946). A *Time Magazine* cover story on Toynbee appeared on March 17, 1947 (pp.29-32), two days after the announcement of the 'Truman Doctrine' calling for aid to Greece and Turkey. The author of the *Time* article was Whittaker Chambers, later famous as the accuser of Alger Hiss.

33. In Siracusa, ed., *The American Diplomatic Revolution*, p.54.

34. George F. Kennan (but published under the pseudonym 'X'), 'The Sources of Soviet Conduct', *Foreign Affairs* XXV (July 1947), p.573, 575, 576.

35. In Siracusa, ed., *The American Diplomatic Revolution*, p.227.

36. Yergin, *Shattered Peace*, p.283.

37. Quoted in Joseph M. Jones, *The Fifteen Weeks* (New York: Harcourt Brace, 1955), p.193.

38. George F. Kennan, *Memoirs, 1925-1950* (Boston: Atlantic Monthly Press, 1967), pp.314-17.

39. Kennan, *Memoirs, 1925-1950*, p.359.

40. Kennan, 'The Sources of Soviet Conduct', p.582.

41. Kennan, *Memoirs, 1925-1950*, p.361.

42. Gaddis, *The Long Peace*, p.48, 49.

43. In Siracusa, ed., *The American Diplomatic Revolution*, p.253, 254, 255.

44. PPS 1 in Thomas Etzold and John Lewis Gaddis, ed., *Containment: Documents on American Policy and Strategy, 1945-1950* (New York: Columbia University Press, 1978), pp.102-3, 104.

45. PPS 1 in Etzold and Gaddis, ed., *Containment*, p.106.

46. See William Taubman, *Stalin's America Policy* (New York: Norton, 1982), pp.172-73.

47. Louis Halle, *The Cold War As History* (New York: Harper and Row, 1967), p.164.

48. Yergin, *Shattered Peace*, p.5.

49. In Etzold and Gaddis, ed., *Containment*, p.66.

50. Walter LaFeber, *America, Russia, and the Cold War 1945-1984* (Fifth edition, New York: Knopf, 1985), p.83.

51. Moscow has now admitted officially what it has denied for four decades — that Fuchs (who had worked on the Manhattan project during the war) did provide the Soviet Union with atomic secrets. See *The Guardian*, August 3, 1988, p.7.

52. NSC-68 in Etzold and Gaddis, ed., *Containment*, p.389, 402.

53. John Lewis Gaddis, *Strategies of Containment: A Critical Appraisal of Postwar American National Security Policy* (New York: Oxford University Press, 1982), pp.114-15.

54. NSC-68 in Etzold and Gaddis, ed., *Containment*, p.426.

55. In A. J. Matusow, ed., *Senator Joseph McCarthy* (Englewood Cliffs: Prentice-Hall, 1970), p.22, 59, 26.

56. See especially, Daniel Bell, ed., *The Radical Right* (New York: Anchor Books, 1964; first published 1955).

57. See E. J. Kahn, *The China Hands: America's Foreign Service Officers and What Befell Them* (New York: Viking, 1975).

58. Owen Lattimore, *Solution in Asia* (Boston: Atlantic Monthly Press, 1945), p.122.

59. Quoted in Kahn, *The China Hands*, pp.174-5.

60. Joseph McCarthy, *America's Retreat From Victory: The Story of George Catlett Marshall* (1952).

61. Foster Rhea Dulles, *American Policy Toward Communist China* (New York: Thomas Crowell, 1972), pp.31-2.

62. *The China White Paper* (Reissued with a new introduction by Lyman van Slyke, Stanford: Stanford University Press, 1967), Volume I, p.xvi.

63. Michael Schaller, *The American Occupation of Japan: The Origins of the Cold War in Asia* (New York: Oxford University Press, 1986), p.51.

64. Schaller, *The American Occupation of Japan*, 51.

65. Schaller, *The American Occupation of Japan*, pp.58-61.

66. See documents 25-34 in Etzold and Gaddis, ed., *Containment*.

67. Schaller, *The American Occupation of Japan*, p.290.

68. Walter Lippmann to Quincy A. Wright, January 23, 1948 in Blum ed., *Public Philosopher: Selected Letters of Walter Lippmann*, p.505.

69. Jacques Rupnik, 'Eastern Europe and the New Cold War', in Crockatt and Smith, eds., *The Cold War Past and Present*, pp.204-5.

70. Michael Cox, 'The Cold War and Stalinism in the Age of Capitalist Decline', *Critique* 17 (1986), pp.17-82.

Guide to Further Reading

Study of American Cold War foreign policy is proceeding with such speed and across such a variety of fronts that the standard surveys inevitably lag some way behind the current state of research. On the question of origins, however, John Lewis Gaddis, *The United States and the Origins of the Cold War, 1941-1947* (New York: Columbia University Press, 1972) and Daniel Yergin, *Shattered Peace: The Origins of the Cold War and the National Security State* (Harmondsworth: Penguin, 1980) have held up well. Yergin offers a more eye-catching thesis and he writes in a more sprightly fashion, but Gaddis's account is judicious and penetrating. Of the many surveys which carry the story forward, in most cases to the 70s and beyond, Walter LaFeber, *America, Russia, and the Cold War, 1945-1984* (5th Edition New York: Knopf, 1985) is a heavily researched revisionist interpretation. Stephen Ambrose, *Rise to Globalism* (Harmondsworth: Penguin, 1988) is readily available in the UK. Among orthodox accounts Louis Halle, *The Cold War as History* (New York: Harper and Row, 1967) contains much which is not to be found elsewhere, particularly on geopolitical issues. Wilfried Loth, *The Division of the World, 1941-1955* (London: Routledge, 1988) is the work of a German historian which offers a fresh perspective upon the scholarly controversies from a relatively detached point of view. Three further books by the ever busy John Lewis Gaddis repay close reading: *Russia, The Soviet Union and the United States: An Interpretive History* (New York: Wiley, 1978); *Strategies of Containment: A Critical Appraisal of Postwar American National Security Policy* (New York: Oxford University Press, 1982); and *The Long Peace: Inquiries into the History of the Cold War* (New York: Oxford University Press, 1987).

The historiographical debate on the Cold War is discussed in Section I of this pamphlet and some of the major works are cited in the text or notes. Among the most useful commentaries on revisionism are Charles Maier, 'Revisionism and the Interpretation of Cold War Origins', *Perspectives in American History* 6 (1970), pp.313-47 and Ole R. Holsti, 'The Study of International Relations Makes Strange Bedfellows: Theories of the Radical Right and the Radical Left', *American Political Science Review*, LXVIII (March 1974), pp.217-42. A useful critique of Williams is J. A. Thompson, 'William Appleman Williams and the 'American Empire', *Journal of American Studies* 7 (1973), pp.91-104. Thomas McCormick, though not restricting his view to the Cold War, has mounted an argument for a new direction in diplomatic history which builds on revisionism and is dismissive of post-revisionism as developed by Gaddis and others. See 'Drift or Mastery? A Corporatist Synthesis for American Diplomatic History', *Reviews in American History*, 10 (December 1982), pp.318-30.

Historians have increasingly sought clues to American policy-making in the cultural and intellectual backgrounds of the policy-makers. Daniel Yergin addresses these issues but Hugh de Santis broke new ground in *The Diplomacy of Silence: The American Foreign Service, The Soviet Union and the Cold War, 1933-47* (Chicago: University of Chicago Press, 1981). Deborah Welch Larsen explores the mind-set of policy-makers in *Origins of Containment: A Psychological Explanation* (Princeton: Princeton University Press, 1985).

Two excellent documentary histories offer a wide range of materials: Joseph M. Siracusa, ed., *The American Diplomatic Revolution: A Documentary History of the Cold War, 1941-1947* (Milton Keynes: Open University Press, 1976); and Thomas Etzold and John Lewis Gaddis, ed., *Containment: Documents on American Policy and Strategy, 1945-1950* (New York: Columbia University Press, 1978).

Of the many memoirs, those by Truman, Acheson, and Byrnes are largely exercises in self-justification and, while important, should be used carefully. George Kennan's two volumes, *Memoirs 1925-1950* (Boston: Atlantic Monthly Press, 1967) and *Memoirs, 1950-63* (London: Hutchinson, 1972), are more reflective and productive of insights as well as being eminently readable. Walter Bedell Smith, *Moscow Mission 1946-1949* (London: Heinemann, 1950) and Charles Bohlen, *Witness to History 1929-1969* (New York: Norton, 1969) contain much interesting detail on life in the Soviet Union as well as diplomatic developments.

It is likely that in the near future knowledge of Soviet policy will be substantially improved. Already several joint American-Soviet working groups are studying aspects of the Cold War. Meanwhile, a number of valuable studies are available: William Taubman, *Stalin's America Policy* (New York: Norton, 1982); Vojtech Mastny, *Russia's Road To the Cold War: Diplomacy, Warfare and the Politics of Communism, 1941-1945* (New York: Columbia University Press, 1979); Adam Ulam, *Expansion and Coexistence: The History of Soviet Foreign Policy, 1917-1967* (New York: Praeger, 1968); and Isaac Deutscher, *Stalin: A Political Biography* (New York: Vintage, 1960), chapters XII-XIV.

Wartime diplomacy is covered in Herbert Feis, *Churchill, Roosevelt and Stalin: The War They Waged and the Peace they Sought* (Princeton: Princeton University Press, 1957); Robert E. Sherwood, *Roosevelt and Hopkins: An Intimate History* (New York: Harper and Row, 1948); Keith Sainsbury, *The Turning Point: Roosevelt, Stalin, Churchill and Chiang Kai-shek, 1943* (Oxford: Oxford University Press, 1986); Robert Dallek, *Franklin Roosevelt and American Foreign Policy, 1932-1945* (New York: Oxford University Press, 1979). Athan Theoharis has charted the political uses made of the 'Yalta myth' by critics of the Roosevelt-Truman policies in *The Yalta Myths: An Issue in American Politics, 1945-1950* (Columbia: University of Missouri Press, 1970). American policy towards Eastern Europe is covered in Lynn Etheridge Davis,

The Cold War Begins (Princeton: Princeton University Press, 1974); Geir Lundstad, *The American Non-Policy Towards Eastern Europe* (Oslo: Univeritestsforlaget, 1978); and Robert Garson, 'The Atlantic Alliance, Eastern Europe and the Origins of the Cold War: From Pearl Harbor to Yalta', in H. C. Allen and Roger Thompson, eds., *Contrast and Connection: Bicentennial Essays in Anglo-American History* (London: G. Bell and Sons, 1976), pp.296-320.

The increasing emphasis on the British role on the early Cold War is well represented by Roy Douglas, *From War to Cold War* (London: Macmillan, 1980); Victor Rothwell, *Britain and the Cold War, 1941-1947* (London: Cape, 1982); Terry Anderson, *The United States, Great Britain, and the Cold War, 1944-1947* (Columbia: University of Missouri Press, 1981) and Fraser Harbutt, *The Iron Curtain: Churchill, America and the Origins of the Cold War* (New York: Oxford University Press, 1986). Alan Bullock's *Ernest Bevin: Foreign Secretary* (London: Heninemann, 1983) is a masterly study.

Economic issues in the US-Soviet relationship are examined from contrasting points of view by Thomas G. Paterson, *Soviet-American Confrontation: Postwar Reconstruction and the Origins of the Cold War* (Baltimore: John Hopkins University Press, 1973) and Robert A. Pollard, *Economic Security and the Origins of the Cold War, 1945-1950* (New York: Columbia University Press, 1985). Paterson finds that the United States was willing to employ economic power for diplomatic leverage, while Pollard concludes that 'postwar American foreign economic policy was not driven by a strong anti-Soviet animus'. Much useful data and analysis is contained in James L. Clayton, ed., *The Economic Impact of the Cold War: Sources and readings* (New York: Harcourt Brace, 1970).

Since the publication in 1965 of Gar Alperovitz's *Atomic Diplomacy: Hiroshima and Potsdam, the Use of the Atomic Bomb and the Confrontation with Soviet Power* (Revised edition, New York: Penguin, 1985) the political implications of atomic weapons in the war against Japan and in relations with the Soviet Union have been the subject of fierce debate. A range of views on these issues is presented in Barton J. Bernstein, ed., *The Atomic Bomb: The Critical Issues* (Boston: Little Brown, 1976). Martin Sherwin, *A World Destroyed: The Atom Bomb and the Grand Alliance* (New York: Vintage Books, 1977) shows that atomic policy was subject to political calculations from the beginning of the Manhattan project. Gregg Herken, *The Winning Weapon: The Atomic Bomb in the Cold War, 1945-1950* (New York: Knopf, 1980) illustrates the illusions governing American policy in the period of its atomic monopoly.

The origins of the Truman Doctrine are covered in the surveys mentioned above. Of great value is Joseph M. Jones, *The Fifteen Weeks*

(New York: Harcourt Brace, 1964), an account by a member of the Truman administration. Bruce Kuniholm's *The Origins of the Cold War in the Near East: Great Power Conflict and Diplomacy in Iran, Greece and Turkey* (Princeton: Princeton University Press, 1980) is the leading study of this subject. Kuniholm makes a strong case for regarding conflict over the 'Northern Tier' of the Middle East as the major breeding ground of the Cold War. Richard Freeland, *The Truman Doctrine and the Origins of McCarthyism* (New York: Knopf, 1972) argues that the seeds of domestic anti-communism were planted by Truman by the manner in which he promoted the Truman Doctrine. On the Marshall Plan see Jones' *Fifteen Weeks* and John Gimbel, *The Origins of the Marshall Plan* (Stanford: Stanford University Press, 1976). Michael J. Hogan's recent book *The Marshall Plan: America, Britain and the Reconstruction of Western Europe, 1947-1952* (Cambridge: Cambridge University Press, 1987) sees American policy as the logical outgrowth of economic assumptions going back to 1920s 'corporatism'. Unlike most studies of the Marshall Plan this one looks in detail at its implementation.

The division of Germany has attracted a good deal of attention from historians, though there is still scope for a study which relates the German issue more widely to the development of the Cold War. Detailed studies of American policy include Bruce Kuklick, *American Policy and the Division of Germany* (Ithaca: Cornell University Press, 1972) and John H. Backer, *The Decision to Divide Germany* (Durham: University of North Carolina Press, 1978). Essays by C. Greiner and N. Wiggershaus in Olav Riste, ed., *Western Security: The Formative Years, European and Atlantic Defence 1947-1953* (Oslo: Norwegian University Press, 1985) examine the issue of German rearmament. The same volume contains essays by L. S. Kaplan, S. F. Wells, Jr and T. H. Etzold on the development of NATO strategy.

Good studies of American Far Eastern policy in the Truman years are Ernest May, *The Truman Administration and China, 1945-49* (New York: Lippincott, 1975) and William W. Stueck, *The Road to Confrontation: American Policy Toward China and Korea, 1947-1950* Chapel Hill: University of North Carolina Press, 1981). In *The China Hands: America's Foreign Service Officers and What Befell Them* (New York: Viking, 1975) E. J. Kahn describes in vivid detail the personal costs borne by America's China specialists in the right wing reaction to the 'loss' of China. Michael Schaller throws much new light on the Cold War in Asia in *The American Occupation of Japan: The Origins of the Cold War in Asia* (New York: Oxford University Press, 1986). Recent research on the origins of the Korean War is synthesized in Peter Lowe, *The Origins of the Korean War* (London: Longman, 1986). Contrasting recent accounts of the war itself, both based on television series, are

Max Hastings, *The Korean War* (London: Michael Joseph, 1987) and Jon Halliday and Bruce Cummings, *Korea: The Unknown War* (New York: Viking, 1988).

On the general phenomenon of anticommunism David Caute's *The Great Fear: The Anticommunist Purge under Truman and Eisenhower* (New York, 1978) is encyclopedic. A useful starting point for McCarthy the man and the 'ism' is Allen J. Matusow, ed., *Senator Joseph McCarthy* (Englewood Cliffs: Prentice-Hall, 1970) which prints some of McCarthy's major speeches, comments by contemporaries, and a range of interpetive studies by historians and sociologists. Richard Rovere's *Senator Joe McCarthy* (New York: Harper and Row, 1973. First published 1959) is an old but still valuable biographical study. Among the best recent biographies is David Oshinsky, *A Conspiracy So Immense: The World of Joe McCarthy* (New York: Free Press, 1982). The debate on the meaning of McCarthyism was set in motion by Daniel Bell, ed., *The Radical Right* (New York: Anchor Books, 1964; first published 1955). Though the sociological assumptions of Bell, Hofstadter et al seem rather dated now, there are hints in this volume which deserve to be taken up, particularly Herbert Hyman's comparative analysis of American and British anti-communism. M. J. Heale carefully tests various theories against the evidence of state politics in 'Red Scare Politics: California's Campaign Against Un-American Activities, 1940-1970', *Journal of American Studies* 20 (April 1986), pp.5-32. On the Hiss case Alistair Cooke's *A Generation on Trial* is an exemplary account of the trial itself while also placing it in historical perspective. Allen Weinstein's massive and controversial *Perjury: The Hiss-Chambers Case* (London: Hutchinson, 1978) should be supplemented by Rhodri Jeffreys-Jones's judicious assessment in 'Weinstein on Hiss', *Journal of American Studies* 13 (April 1979), pp.115-26.

BAAS PAMPHLETS IN AMERICAN STUDIES

1. **SLAVERY**
   by Peter J. Parish
2. **PROGRESSIVISM**
   by J. A. Thompson
3. **THE PRESIDENT AND THE SUPREME COURT: NEW DEAL TO WATERGATE**
   by John D. Lees
4. **THE METROPOLITAN MOSAIC: PROBLEMS OF THE CONTEMPORARY CITY**
   by Philip Davies
5. **THE COMIC SELF IN POST-WAR AMERICAN FICTION**
   by Stan Smith
6. **THE AMERICAN DREAM**
   by Robert H. Fossum and John K. Roth
7. **THE WELFARE STATE IN AMERICA, 1930-1980**
   by James T. Patterson
8. **MODERN INDIANS: NATIVE AMERICANS IN THE TWENTIETH CENTURY**
   by David Murray
9. **THE EXPATRIATE TRADITION IN AMERICAN LITERATURE**
   by Malcolm Bradbury
10. **THE IMMIGRANT EXPERIENCE IN AMERICAN LITERATURE**
    by Edward A. Abramson
11. **BLACK AMERICAN FICTION SINCE RICHARD WRIGHT**
    By A. Robert Lee
12. **AMERICAN PHOTOGRAPHY**
    by Mick Gidley
13. **THE PEOPLE'S AMERICAN REVOLUTION**
    by Edward Countryman
14. **EMILY DICKINSON AS AN AMERICAN PROVINCIAL POET**
    by Michael Allen
15. **BRITISH AMERICA, 1607-1763**
    by W. A. Speck
16. **HOLLYWOOD**
    by Brian Lee
17. **NATHANIEL HAWTHORNE**
    by David Timms
18. **THE UNITED STATES AND THE COLD WAR 1941-53**
    by Richard Crockatt

Pamphlets may be purchased from Lofthouse Publications, 29 Ropergate, Pontefract, West Yorkshire WF8 1LG.